OCTAVES *of* SUCCESS

88 KEYS TO A PASSION-CENTERED CAREER

Meg,
Make sure to follow
your passions! :-)

NEWELL H. HILL

ISBN: 978-0-9891111-0-2
Library of Congress Number: 2013904297

Printed in the United States of America
First Printing: 2013

Book cover and layout, designed by:
Annie Johnson, www.designlovelife.com

Moon Landing Press, Inc.
125 E Main Street
Belle Plaine, MN 56011

To order visit **www.octavesofsuccess.com**
Or call (651) 343-4703. Reseller Discounts available.

TABLE of CONTENTS

DEDICATED TO TEACHERS WHO HELP THEIR STUDENTS BELIEVE IN THEMSELVES AND INSPIRE THEM TO BE BETTER THAN THEY THOUGHT THEY COULD BE.

INTRODUCTION

O ur society has reached a point where we no longer sit idly by and tolerate careers that bring little joy or sense of accomplishment to our lives. With more freedom than ever, we now choose how we earn a living and spend the majority of our short time here on earth. True happiness lies not at the bottom of a Mai-tai martini glass on a surf-drenched beach, but instead in doing real, meaningful work that CONNECTS us to our passions. A growing swell of new possibilities and new thinking redefines traditional attitudes towards careers, life, and passion. We now connect our careers with our passions and wash away the old and tired lines in the sand. Our passions and our careers have become one and the same.

At the age of nineteen, I connected my passion for music and helping kids by starting a nonprofit that sells donated pianos to raise money for an after-school program called MUSE (Music Understanding in a Supportive Environment). I'm now thirty-two, and over the last thirteen years, I have had many experiences and learned numerous lessons while creating a career that aligns with my passions and interests. I am writing this book because

I want to share these experiences with you and help YOU create a career that aligns with YOUR passions.

Organized like the keyboard of a piano, this book contains eighty-eight keys, or lessons, that share various experiences I have had while fixing, moving, and selling pianos. I have also structured the book into octaves, with each octave containing twelve keys. Each octave represents a different phase in the process of connecting your passions to a fulfilling and rewarding career. I hope to guide, encourage, and inspire you on your journey to create a Passion-Centered Career (PCC).

· · · · · · · · · ·

I have read many self-help and motivational books. While writing this book, I borrowed some of the techniques and styles of my favorite authors. I have written this book in a way that I, as a reader, would enjoy and appreciate.

I like books that organize ideas and concepts into manageable, concise sections that make a point as well as work together as a whole to explain a broader message.

This book contains eight-eight keys or sections, which individually explain specific points and ideas but that also work together to guide you while you discover and realize your PCC. These keys are individual notes, but together, they create beautiful music and harmony in your life. Similar to how lower notes on a keyboard are the bass notes, the first keys in this book are intended to give you a "base" or foundation on which to build a rewarding career. The progression of keys is ordered in a way that will guide and inspire you in this transformation process.

I also like books that tell stories. I love when authors share anecdotes and introduce characters to explain a message.

I have done this in my book by telling stories and experiences from my own life. I hope these stories help bring some depth and color to my messages as well as make your reading experience more enjoyable.

Lastly, I like when authors provide space and invite me to share my own thoughts and ideas. Reading can be a passive process, and I want to invite you to engage and participate as much as possible. I have incorporated several places throughout the book to write down and share your ideas.

. . . .

PREFACE

I grew up in a suburb of St. Paul, Minnesota called Woodbury. I like to play golf, fly single-engine airplanes, and sail. I am also the founder of a nonprofit organization that accepts and sells donated pianos for charity called Keys 4/4 Kids (K44K). K44K currently has warehouse locations in St. Paul, Chicago, and Kansas City. I started K44K in my parents' basement in 2000 in order to raise money for an after-school program in Minneapolis called MUSE. I developed the curriculum for MUSE around the philosophy that learning music should be a fun, positive experience available to everyone.

My sister and I took piano lessons as children, but I hated to practice. In the 7th grade, I finally talked my mom into letting me stop taking lessons.

A couple of years later, I started playing the piano for fun, and I came up with my own chord combinations that eventually turned into songs. I didn't think much of it, but pretty soon, I had composed several minutes of completely original music. I kept writing music and played the piano for several hours every day.

Around the same time, I had an inspirational high-school teacher named Mrs. Conway. She encouraged her students to go out into the world and help others less fortunate. I can still remember her coming to tears almost every day, telling us stories of how people throughout history have made great sacrifices so others can lead better lives. Whether we learned about Harriet Tubman and her underground railroad to free slaves, or the lives lost fighting a ruthless dictator in WWII, the message remained the same: go into this world and make a positive difference for others. Her influence gave me the inspiration to share my love of music with kids who might not otherwise be able to afford lessons.

As a freshman at the University of Minnesota (U of M) I volunteered as part of a big-buddy program called Y-Buddies, a program through the University YMCA (U-Y). During my time there, I learned about another program at the U-Y called Y-Tutors, which sent college students into schools to tutor kids in math and reading. On the second floor of the U-Y, a wall of bookshelves housed binders of curricula for teaching kids to read and solve math problems, but not one binder existed to teach kids about music and art. I saw an opportunity to create a program that gave low-income students the opportunity to learn a musical instrument.

I remember going to the U-Y on a sunny spring day to propose a new music-and-arts-based curriculum for the Y-Tutors program. I met with the coordinator of the Y-Tutors program, Eric. Eric had straight, light-blond hair, always wore a smile, and he loved to make people laugh.

I enthusiastically told Eric all of my ideas about creating a program that made learning a musical instrument fun and engaging. I wanted to incorporate art projects into the program so kids would have several things engaging their creativity. I told Eric about how I had enjoyed playing the violin in the Minnesota Youth Symphonies when I was growing up and how I wanted to incorporate the idea of creating music as a group into my curriculum. I also told him about how I wanted to focus on the playing styles and genres of music that interested the students. I didn't like playing the piano when I took lessons because I played music I didn't like. I wanted to teach kids to create music that they would appreciate.

After listening to me, a tall, gangly college student with bushy curly hair for about thirty minutes, Eric finally shook my hand, smiled, and told me he would make it happen. He told me he could arrange for fifteen volunteers from the Y-Tutors program to teach with me in the following school year. We decided to call the program MUSE. I remember the feeling of excitement as I skipped back to my dorm room.

. . . .

During that summer, I began preparing curriculum for MUSE and tried to think of ways to raise money for art supplies and instruments.

One idea I had involved producing a CD of my original piano music. By this time, I had written more than fifteen songs, which was more than enough music for a CD.

I called around to local music studios to find a place to record. I eventually found a guy who had a studio in his basement, and I set up my first recording appointment. I practiced for several hours the day before and planned to record only two or three songs.

When I arrived at his split-level house in a suburban neighborhood, I took off my shoes, and the owner introduced himself as Jim. He was a gruff, overweight middle-aged man. He smiled at me and asked if I had ever been to a recording studio. I told him I had not, and he looked at me with a squint in his eye, as if to say, *ok, kid, let's see what you got.*

We walked down the stairs to his basement, where I saw his beautiful, black, polished grand piano. There was only one window in the whole basement and it streamed afternoon sunlight. Jim told me the glass in the window was more than two inches thick, to prevent street noise.

Jim used DAT tapes (similar to cassette tapes, only larger) for the music he recorded. He crumpled the noisy clear plastic that wrapped one of these DAT cases, threw it in a trash can, and walked to another room.

I explored the piano a little further. Three large microphones, encased in silver mesh, dove under the lid of the grand piano. The microphones hovered centimeters above the strings, ready to capture the slightest touch of my fingers.

11 | OCTAVES *of* SUCCESS

Jim sat behind a large window, surrounded by electronic equipment, blinking lights, and spinning wheels. Jim looked at me, a red light turned on above him, and he pointed at me. A dense cloud of silence floated through the room.

My hands were wet with sweat and my fingers trembled with nervousness. I rubbed my hands quietly against my pants and brought my hands back to the keyboard. I took a deep, long breath. I played the first note, then the second. Notes began to come alive, and together they created music.

Then, a mistake.

I waited for Jim to reset the DAT tape, the light to turn on, and for him to once again point to me.

I went back to this studio several times, playing each song over and over until I had recorded it with no mistakes. Within three months, all my songs were digitalized and ready for production!

I brought my "master" to a company that designed a cover and produced 1,000 CDs for around $2,000. I would load my car with these CDs, a small folding card table, a battery-powered CD player, and I sold the CDs for $10 at fairs and conventions. I even had a cardboard display made out of construction paper and glue that said "give the gift of music."

Over the next year, I sold all 1,000 CDs, and I used the money to support MUSE.

· · · · · · · · · ·

Another idea I had to raise money for MUSE came to me at a garage sale in my hometown of Woodbury. It was the summer after my freshman year of college, and my friend Steve and I were out bargain shopping. We came across an old piano with a price tag of $50. At the time, I knew nothing about how pianos worked, but I wanted to learn. I loved the fact that pianos were made from wood and metal, and everything was so mechanical. I also liked the fact that this piano was more than 100 years old: it had history and character. I thought if I brought the piano back to my parents' house, I could fix it up and sell it for more money.

I told the owner of the piano that I wanted it and I would be back later that day. Steve had a lawn and landscape business, and he let me borrow the trailer he used to pull a riding lawnmower to the yards of his customers. We went back to his house, put the trailer behind an old minivan with no rear seats, but plenty of grass clippings, rakes, and hedge trimmers bouncing around the back seat, and we picked up the old piano.

It took us some time to get the piano loaded and tied down. It teetered back and forth as straps blew in the wind while we carefully delivered it to my parents' house.

When we arrived, a new business had been born.

I didn't touch the piano the first day. It sat in a large room underneath a three-car garage we called "the dungeon." As a child, I had used the dungeon to build go-carts and harvest wood left by the previous owners to build a tree fort in the backyard. My dad used it for his woodworking projects, but he often yielded to the chaos of my latest project.

I walked down the basement stairs the following morning and opened the garage door of the dungeon. As I opened the garage door, streams of sunlight bounced off the dust as it floated through the air.

I opened the front of the piano and saw all the wooden pieces fit together in perfect rows. I wondered if I would ever understand how they all worked together to create sound. I imagined the lives of the carpenters who constructed it so many years ago.

I felt a responsibility to fix and bring life back into these old worn parts. I could hardly contain my excitement to reach into this piano and tighten screws, clamp broken wood pieces, and replace parts. Tarnished metal hinges, aching with age and arthritis, still clung to their wood counterparts, stoic and determined to once again create beautiful, rich music, only ripened with age.

I bought manuals and books that told me how to fix and tune pianos. Before I knew it, I had filled the dungeon with old, forgotten pianos, and I put ads in local newspapers advertising the pianos for sale.

Me posing for a newspaper article in 1999 at the age of nineteen.
I had recently started K44K in my parents' basement.

During that first summer, I sold a little over $10,000 worth of pianos. My parents helped move them, and I continued to use the same old motorcycle trailer pulled behind a red Saturn sedan. Piano sales surpassed my CD sales many times over, mostly because competition to be a musician is fierce, whereas no one sells used pianos for charity. You will increase your chances for success if you separate yourself from others and therefore reduce competition (and I'll talk more about this later in the book).

Over the coming years, I continued to sell pianos out of my parents' basement; I also applied for grants from local corporations and foundations to support MUSE. By my junior year in college, I had a board of directors and about twenty staff; I had received more than $100,000 from grants and donations; and I oversaw MUSE in three schools and taught music and art to more than 120 kids annually.

During my junior year, while standing at the front of a campus connector bus, clinging to one of the metal poles bolted to the floor and ceiling, I watched the wiper blades chase each other while swiping rain beads on the windshield. I was on my way to math class on the west bank and suddenly connected the dots and saw the possibility that THIS could be my job. Until then, I had only seen MUSE as a fun project, a way to engage my passions until I graduated and got a REAL job. I felt a flutter of excitement rise up from inside me as I suddenly saw my life and my career in such a different, more exciting perspective.

For the next few years, I devoted myself full-time to my nonprofit. I improved our curriculum and held silent art show fundraisers every fall. I had an office at the U-Y and held meetings with my four coordinators every Wednesday. I felt challenged and rewarded every day. I saw the pride on the face of Julie, a volunteer staff member, as she raised her usually quiet and meek voice to get the attention of a room full of energized 2nd graders. I saw a student named Lauren show up early to class in order to get a head start on her African-mask project.

At the time, I took only a small salary from the business, and I lived at home with my parents to save money. Now in my early twenties, I felt pressure from society to be "successful." I thought I should have a nice car, my own place, and of course, more money. Although running a nonprofit connected with my passions, I fell into a trap of wanting a stereotypical, superficial concept of success. So I hired someone to replace me and started investing in real estate.

The person I hired to replace me had a difficult time renewing grants from foundations and corporations that had given us grants in the past. We later realized that these donors were giving grants to ME, because they believed in ME. When I no longer went to these meetings to request money, they stopped funding our program. Only two years after I left, we had to close the doors to MUSE.

After I left MUSE, I did find traditional success in real estate. I bought a Mercedes and had a lot of money to spend on nice things, but in the end, I only found boredom and unhappiness.

I eventually returned to my passion-filled career in 2009. I rebuilt my nonprofit with a focus on raising money through the piano sales. I no longer wanted to depend on donors renewing their grants each year. I also started my own for-profit piano-moving business called Econo Piano Move (EPM).

In the past, K44K had always paid a separate piano-moving company to do our moves, but I wanted to have more control over these moves. I also thought I could save K44K money by charging it less money. Also, forming EPM allowed me to work on K44K full-time because I could take a salary from EPM and continue to work for K44K as a volunteer.

Today, we no longer support MUSE, but hope to again in coming years, and for now, we have four other programs that support our mission to *inspire kids to believe in themselves through the arts and mentorship.*

- The *Piano Placement Program* gives pianos away for free to low-income families.

- *Pianos on Parade* pairs local artists with students and has them paint pianos together. After the pianos are 'artistically transformed,' they are placed in outdoor locations during the summer for the public to play and enjoy.

- The *Paint a Piano* program is similar to Pianos on Parade, only we bring pianos into churches, community centers, and schools for kids to paint.

- The *Maureen Conway "I Inspire Kids to Believe in Themselves" Award* is a monetary gift given to teachers who help *awaken the potential that already exists within their students and help them be better than they thought they could be.* I created this award in honor of my high school history teacher, Maureen Conway, who helped me to believe in myself.

I am excited to go to work every single day. I learned that money and nice things will bring you happiness and fulfillment for a short time, but eventually, you will be left feeling empty and frustrated. I am glad each and every day because I get to do something I love. I have worked for money and I have worked for something I believe in, and I am much happier when I work for things I believe in. If you do things you believe in, you will do them well and money will follow close behind.

OCTAVE 1:

DISCOVER AND TRUST YOU

"YOU'VE GOT TO FOLLOW YOUR PASSION. YOU'VE GOT TO FIGURE OUT WHAT IT IS YOU LOVE—WHO YOU REALLY ARE. AND HAVE THE COURAGE TO DO THAT. I BELIEVE THAT THE ONLY COURAGE ANYBODY EVER NEEDS IS THE COURAGE TO FOLLOW YOUR OWN DREAMS."

-OPRAH WINFREY

1. SLOW DOWN AND CREATE SPACE

When in high school and later college, I always felt this intense sense of urgency. It seemed people couldn't graduate fast enough, get high enough grades, or impress enough people along the way. Our current education system creates an incredibly competitive, fast-paced, and hectic environment; this is not an ideal climate to nurture, discover, and encourage the development of an individual's talents, interests, and passions.

I want you to know that *you have time.* You don't have to get sucked into the hectic environment of an educational institution or any environment that doesn't allow you the space and freedom to discover YOU.

The education system churns out students like a factory assembly line. You are not a product. You are a unique individual who has gifts and talents that need to be discovered and nurtured. This takes time and patience. Give yourself permission to take this time and create this space.

The process of taking this time will look different for everyone. It might mean taking a year for yourself before you enter college, or maybe it will mean not declaring a major in your first year. Maybe you will not take twenty credits, but instead take eight next semester.

I want you to know you can take a breath. Even if everyone around you seems frantic, and it seems like you are going to get behind, you won't. You will find more success and happiness in your life when your career aligns with your talents and passions. If you rush into a career that isn't right for you, you will be miserable and eventually quit.

2. MAKE A LIST OF THINGS THAT BRING YOU JOY

You probably already have some ideas about things that bring you joy. Maybe it's photography or music. Maybe it's watching a movie or hanging out with friends. Don't worry about turning them into a career right now.

I want you to write a list of things that give you JOY. These are things you can't wait to do when you get out of class or that you stay up late doing. Things that bring you joy will engage you and challenge your physical, mental, and creative capabilities.

You may have done these things since you were three, or you might have never tried them. List them ALL.

I want to help you attract more JOY into your life, in richer and more fulfilling ways than you ever thought possible.

1. _____

2. _____

3. _____

4. _____

5. _____

6. _____

7. _____

8. _____

3. TRY NEW THINGS

During my freshman year in college, I desperately wanted to be "successful." I had been good at math and science in high school, so it made sense for me to be a doctor. I took a lot of difficult, pre-med courses and tried to get the best grades I could. Hope and optimism filled the air as the leaves changed colors during the fall of my first semester at the U of M.

Soon I started getting papers and quizzes back with scores much lower than I had hoped. My grades continued to slip, and I wanted to quit. My goal of becoming a doctor seemed impossible, and I didn't know where to turn.

Thankfully, I became involved with the U-Y and the Y-Buddies program during my freshman year. This program offered me a chance to take my mind off my horrible, depressing grades and the difficulty I was having working toward my goal to become a doctor. I had a chance to work with other caring, motivated college students, and I immersed myself in a new, more opportunity-filled world.

The program paired college students with at-risk youth from Minneapolis. Y-Buddies showed these kids that someone cares about them and someone WANTS to spend time with them. Love and attention ran in short supply, and this program gave kids the encouragement they needed.

Although I thought I wanted to be a doctor, trying new things helped me find opportunities that more closely aligned with my own talents and passions.

List a few things you may want to try:

1. _____

2. _____

3. _____

4. _____

5. _____

6. _____

7. _____

8. _____

4. TRAVEL

Are you having trouble finding things that bring you joy? Consider a trip! I believe our surroundings have a lot to do with how we think. If your environment stays the same, it's hard to have original or new ideas. Trips are a great way to see and experience the world in new ways and to hopefully generate ideas and insight.

I saw an interview last night with the last astronaut to walk on the moon. He talked about how perfect the Earth looked while he stood on the moon. He described how the blues from the ocean, greens and browns from the ground, and whites from the clouds all mixed and swirled together like abstract art. He said the Earth seemed to move with a resolute, destined, and divine purpose. It became a spiritual experience for him as he stood there observing such beauty, perfection, and absoluteness.

I have never been to the moon, but I recently traveled to Paris. My plane left in the evening, and soon after takeoff, the lights in the cabin dimmed. As our plane raced across the Atlantic Ocean, I got up to walk around and stretch my legs. I went to the back of the plane and looked out a nearby window, and I saw the sun rising out of the ocean skyline as slivers of light danced across the corners of the cabin.

I have never seen a more beautiful sunrise. I met this new day somewhere in the Mid-Atlantic. I may have been the only person on earth witnessing the sunrise at this moment. My watch said only 11PM, and my body knew the morning should not be here so soon, but my eyes and heart welcomed this new day.

When we landed in Paris, the round clock on the terminal gate, covered in a glass dome, read 6AM. I quietly glided on an electric train through the early morning countryside, into the depths of the city through an underground channel. I walked up the stairs leading to a main street, only to be greeted by a lonely street sweeper. I strolled down the empty, twisting roads, wanting to find my hotel, but I was also excited to see this beautiful city.

I saw shop owners opening local bread and pastry shops, and I stopped by one that faced a fountain in the middle of a large open space. Still too early for the sounds of gurgling water, the pool of water calmly waited for the day to begin while suspended in time, as long elongated shadows from nearby buildings draped the surrounding square.

I went into the shop and asked for a croissant in broken French, and I sat by the fountain. To most people in Paris that day, nothing seemed new or out of the ordinary. For my eyes, though, everything seemed new. Everything tasted as fresh and as delicious as the croissant I held in my hand.

Traveling challenges our perception of the world. Traveling peels back the layers of our perceived reality and forces us to reexamine our old beliefs. Our brains want to understand and control, and by mastering our small, isolated corner of the world, we smother our creativity and potential. Traveling gives fresh meaning, perspective, and connection to a big wonderful world.

List a few places you want to travel:

1. _____

2. _____

3. _____

4. _____

5. _____

6. _____

7. _____

8. _____

5. REMEMBER, MONEY IS NOT A PASSION

Take money off your list of passions. Passions connect you with your TALENTS and GIFTS; money is a tool to make these connections, but it's not a passion.

I fell into this trap when I thought I wanted to be rich. At the time, I no longer ran MUSE and had recently got my realtor license. Within three months I flipped three houses and made over $200,000. I bought a brand-new Mercedes and moved into a nice apartment.

I stayed up late, went to bars, and slept in until noon. I did this day after day, for two years. This might sound like a great life, but I promise you, it was not. I did not do things that connected with my talents and passions; I spent money.

One night, I invited my friend Gregg over to my apartment. When he arrived, I went down to the front door of the apartment building to meet him. We gave each other a hug; I think it had been over a year since I saw him last. The main entrance of the apartment building had a marble floor and a large flat-screen TV displaying the local weather. We walked by the courtyard that had huge planting pots filled with trees and flowers.

My apartment had brand-new wood floors and high, vaulted ceilings. I had some of my own abstract paintings hanging on two of the walls. One of the walls was completely covered in windows and faced the courtyard.

Gregg had served on my board of directors when I ran MUSE and, although he wouldn't tell me in words, I could see the disappointment in his eyes. I had lost the connection to my PCC. I no longer stood for something good or more important than myself. I had become what I thought society wanted me to be, but this mold did not represent me.

I asked Gregg if he wanted a drink. The top of my shelves were stocked with all kinds of alcohol. The bottles clanked against each other as I grabbed a bottle of vodka. Almost every night, I had a vodka cranberry drink in the hot tub directly below my balcony window.

Gregg and I sat on my couch and talked for a while. We talked about how my monthly expenses exceeded $8,000. Gregg told me his budget for fun money was only $10 per day.

That week, I had about $10,000 in cash in the apartment, rolled up with a rubber band. I had recently taken the money out of my bank, just for fun. Later that week, one of my friends, Robbie, brought it to the bar to impress girls. I don't know if it impressed them or not, but it made me nervous having it passed around a dark bar.

Eventually, Gregg asked me one of his deep, introspective questions about life, and I took a little too long to answer. He accused me of being too drunk to have a conversation with him.

It was true.

During these two years in this fancy apartment, I was too drunk on alcohol, money, and THINGS to have any kind of meaning in my life. Looking back, I realize these were unhappy years in my life.

6. DEFINE YOUR IDEAL DAY

When you imagine your ideal day, what does it look like? Where do you wake up? What is the first thing you do in the morning? Who are you with and what happens throughout the day?

You can have several ideal days. Maybe one is a day filled with fun. You do something exciting with your friends, or you go someplace you have never been. It can be extravagant and expensive, or whatever you like it to be.

Now imagine a day filled with pride and accomplishment. What have you accomplished? Who have you had an impact on? Who is there to celebrate with you?

Describe a day filled with fun:

_____

_____

_____

_____

_____

_____

Describe a day filled with pride:

_____

_____

_____

_____

_____

_____

After you have described these two different days, pick the one that excites you the most. Close your eyes and visualize and experience that day right now, in the present. Imagine how you feel, what you smell, what you hear. Picture yourself in the moment.

It's easy to get overwhelmed by the complexity of achieving a goal, but you can break your goal down into smaller, more manageable parts.

My ideal day involved sailing a wooden boat on White Bear Lake. I could hear the waves crashing on the boat hull, and I could see the sea gulls floating overhead. I imagined taking my friends on the boat, packing lunches and fishing rods, and enjoying a windy summer day. I imagined it so clearly and it felt so real that it propelled me to work more than 2,000 hours on this

A clear vision and defined ideal day will help overcome any obstacle and achieve the impossible.

Me next to a 17' sailboat I designed and built in 1999.

7. LISTEN TO YOUR INNER VOICE

I believe there is a tiny voice inside you, guiding you with challenges and decisions in your life. Sometimes it's more of a feeling, like gears of bicycle clicking into place, than a voice. When you are doing something that aligns with your passions, it feels right.

When you do something that does not align with your passions, you will know this as well. Sometimes I have trouble breathing. I might not be aware anything is wrong, but if this happens, I know something needs my attention or I need to make a change in my life.

Sometimes I feel pressure behind my eyes. It's hard for me to keep my eyes open, and they burn. I know if I have this feeling, I am doing something that is not "in tune" with my passions and talents. I have these feelings if I spend too much time doing office work, balancing budgets, or spackling sheetrock, for instance.

These physical sensations give me clues, like signs along a road that point in the direction of my PCC. When I used to play the piano, I would lose track of time. I would play for hours and not realize how long I had played. When I finally finished, my entire body became relaxed and calm.

It's simple. Do the things that your body tells you feel right, and *don't* do the things that feel forced. It takes courage to say "no" to the things that sap your energy and "yes" to the things that *give* you energy.

Trust yourself.

8. EVOLVE

I rarely play the piano anymore. I have tried to sit down and write music like I used to, but I don't enjoy it now. Lots of people tell me that I should play more, but it's no longer one of my passions. My passion now involves growing my business and expanding the work of our mission.

We all change and evolve over time, and we should accept this about ourselves. When I was five, I thought a fictional cartoon character named He-Man was pretty much the best thing in the world. I would put toys in my underwear and run around the house because I wanted to be just like him.

The things you enjoy doing today may be boring tomorrow. You owe it to yourself to be true to your CURRENT passions. There are no passion police who will make you do one thing for the rest of our life.

So what are you excited about TODAY?

1. _____

2. _____

3. _____

4. _____

5. _____

6. _____

7. _____

8. _____

9. DON'T STRESS OUT ABOUT GRADES

I wish I had realized this key in high school: it would have saved me a lot of stress. I used to worry so much about some random grade on a test or paper. My stress level would be sky high when I got papers and tests graded. I worried about how one test would affect my grade for the semester, and how that semester grade would affect my GPA for the year, and how that GPA would affect what college I would attend, and how that college would affect my entire future happiness and success.

Realizing success in your PCC depends more on a positive attitude than your GPA.

RELAX.

I remember feeling jealous that my sister had better grades and was on track to take more advanced classes in high school. I used to think she was so lucky and was in the perfect position to find success in life.

My friend Andy got a much higher score than I did on the SAT. He knew all the big words on the verbal section, words I had never heard of, and he scored high on math as well. I remember lying on a hammock under the deck at my parents' house while I talked to him on the phone about our test scores. After I found out how high he scored, I hung up the phone and closed my eyes. I felt waves of jealousy crash over me. I thought about how many more options Andy had for colleges. I felt I would miss out on life because of a couple of test scores.

But when I went down to the office of the Secretary of State to incorporate my business, no one asked me for my high school transcript or SAT score.

Having a high GPA and SAT scores are not bad things, and I would recommend taking advantage of every learning opportunity you have while in high school, but don't stress out about these numbers or grades being indicators of future success.

If I was going to pick some ACTUAL indicators of success, I would say you should have:

1. A defined direction or goal.
2. The ability to organize time and energy efficiently.
3. The ability to take action.

10. CHANGE YOUR TRUTH

We all have a system of beliefs or truths that affect our decisions and behaviors in a subconscious way. These truths can be formed from an experience we had or maybe a comment someone said to us.

In middle school, I didn't have friends at school so I usually sat alone at the lunch tables. The other kids would call me a "loser," and this label stuck. I did things to make sure I WAS a loser. I didn't try hard in school, and I didn't want to do well in anything. I still struggle with this today, and sometimes I find myself resisting success.

In high school, I found permission for the first time to break this cycle. I had a teacher named Mrs. Conway who believed in me. She met with me between classes and helped me with papers and history assignments. She helped change the truth I had about myself. I started to believe in myself.

Having one person believe in me changed the way I thought about myself. I hope you have someone like this in your life. If not, YOU need to be the one who gives yourself permission to believe.

So say to yourself quietly, but with persistence, "I believe in myself."

Maureen Conway and Newell Hill in 2013.

11. EMBRACE FAILURE

Fear of failure has stopped many talented and driven people.

Some fear is good, of course. You should be afraid to jump off a building or drive your car with no brakes. But fear of failure, approval, or the unfamiliar create heavy, stubborn burdens that hold you back and prevent you from reaching your full potential.

In 2006, while working as a real estate investor, values of properties suddenly plummeted. I owed more money on the houses than they were worth. I remember sitting in my apartment one night, surrounded by my nice things and fancy clothes, knowing I could no longer afford this lifestyle. I remember the FEAR of losing all these THINGS. These things had become ingrained in my identity. I WAS my Mercedes. I WAS my fancy clothes. I truly felt that if I lost these things, I would cease to exist.

At the time, K44K operated out of a small storefront in South Minneapolis. In order to save money I sold my car and moved into the basement of the K44K store. There was no hot water and no shower. It was winter and I had several space heaters, but the concrete floors were still cold. I slept on moving blankets, and I hung my clothes from rafters in the ceiling.

After a few weeks of living in the basement, I started to develop new routines, and my life started to stabilize. I had a large green leather chair nestled in the corner of this small square basement. The chair had several tears, and stuffing gushed from these openings like the sugary filling of an overcooked cherry pie. I could reach out and touch the work bench I used to repair piano parts and tools dangled on the wall behind me.

Because I could no longer afford to go to bars or restaurants, I spent most nights in this old green chair. The low rattles of springs clanging and the high-pitched squeaks of rubbing metal replaced the cacophony of subwoofers and loud voices of an alcohol-infused club.

I had a small table with a tall red lamp next to the chair. It was made from a deep crimson fabric and had fringe dangling from the bottom. It glowed a warm red hue and made the cement-encased room seem cozy. As I sat in this chair one night, I had a moment of great insight. I realized a simple, but profound fact.

I was OK.

No, really: I had never felt better. I felt ALIVE and FREE. I realized in this moment that I was still the same person I have always been. In fact, I was even more in touch with my true identity because I didn't have all this STUFF and expensive DISTRACTIONS crowding my life.

From this new perspective, I could better appreciate all the beauty and simple miracles of the world around me. I discovered new books and saw each moment as a fresh and new discovery. I became present.

12. BELIEVE IN YOURSELF

So by this point, you should have a few ideas of things that bring you JOY, right?

I think for most people, thinking of things that bring them joy is the easy part; the challenge comes when they are asked to turn them into a career. I want to help you find a creative solution that turns your passions into a career. When you find a creative solution, unique and personalized to your passions, several things happen:

1. You have less competition from others trying to do something similar, so you increase your chances of success.
2. You have greater control over your career and therefore more freedom in your life.
3. You will truly love your career because it is specific to your own passions and talents.

If your passion involves teaching kids, what EXACTLY about teaching kids draws you to this interest? Whatever that is, specialize in it, enhance it, focus on it, and do it better than anyone else.

For me, I wanted to use the arts to teach kids to believe in themselves. I created the MUSE curriculum around this passion, and in doing this, I opened many doors of opportunity.

Fear keeps people from focusing on the specific thing that draws them to their passion. It takes confidence to forge your own path. I want you to know you don't need skill, ability, or even a shred of evidence to have the confidence needed to forge your own path.

All you need is to *believe in yourself.*

During high school, I had so many papers to write. Some assignments would be about books we had read and some were about our perspective on a historical event or person. I wrote several papers for Mrs. Conway, and I don't think I ever did better than B work. Writing never came easily for me.

For most of 11th-grade English, I gave only a moderate amount of effort. The books we read didn't interest me, and the fact that my papers always came back with grades of C and C- didn't inspire me to put much effort into the next one. One day, however, I decided I would try, really try. I think I wanted to prove to myself that I could write an A paper if I truly put my mind to it.

The assignment involved writing a report on a poem by Edgar Allen Poe. I chose the story about a pendulum swinging in a cave. It made little sense to me at the time, and still, to this day, I don't understand why there was a pendulum swinging in that stupid cave.

Over a long weekend, I sat with a computer in my room and typed out a rough draft. I found references and cited them. I reread and proofread. I even asked my friend Andy to come over and help me. I have never put so much effort into a writing project in my life.

When I got the assignment back the following week, my teacher had given me a B-. I hadn't cried since the 1st grade, but I cried in the upper school hallway that day. I felt so frustrated and defeated.

I am telling you this because I have no good reason to think I have any talent or ability to write or be an author, yet here I am, typing these words on this page. If my high-school English teacher thought any of his students would go on to become published authors, I guarantee I would be one of the last on his list.

I am writing this book because I have a story to tell and a powerful message to share. Writing is a tool to share this story with others. I believe in myself, and I believe I can write a book.

You too can believe in yourself, and you don't need to get an A or even one shred of hard evidence to justify that.

Me sitting at a painted piano in 2010.

OCTAVE 2:

QUALITIES FOR SUCCESS

"SUCCESS IS THE SUM OF SMALL EFFORTS,
REPEATED DAY AFTER DAY."

-ROBERT COLLIER, EARLY 20TH CENTURY
AMERICAN AUTHOR

1. KNOW YOUR STRENGTHS & WEAKNESSES

Do you hear a common theme in the compliments you receive from friends and family? Maybe how outgoing or funny you are? Maybe it's that you are diligent and hardworking? Whatever your talents, you will need to leverage these skills for your PCC.

When I believe something can work, or when I'm excited to try something new, I usually *go for it*. I don't need to think through all the ways an idea can succeed or fail before I try it. This can be an asset when starting a business. Instead of worrying about how it might fail, I have the confidence in myself to figure it out.

Too much confidence can also be a weakness. Sometimes, I am wrong about obstacles I can overcome. When this happens, my decisions seem impulsive and reckless. I once made a $16,000 down-payment on a condo because I thought I could afford the $4,000 per month mortgage payment. I designed the entire layout down to the grout color in the bathroom and never slept there one night.

My over-confidence cost money in this situation.

When I started the business to sell pianos out of my parents' house, I didn't have all the answers. I did, however, have confidence that I could figure them out and solve problems that might arise. This confidence helped me build a business that has sold more than 1 million dollars worth of used pianos.

By understanding my tendency towards impulsive decisions, I put a policy in place to run any big decisions by a group of advisors who I know and trust. Embracing and utilizing your unique skills and personality will help create success, but you must also recognize how these characteristics may cause you to stumble.

What are your strengths?

1. _____

2. _____

3. _____

4. _____

5. _____

6. _____

7. _____

8. _____

How may these strengths cause you to stumble?

1. _____

2. _____

3. _____

4. _____

5. _____

6. _____

7. _____

8. _____

2. SELF-TEACH

Because your career path is a creative process, your education should be specific and creative as well. It will take discipline and commitment, but the rewards will be worth it.

Books are a great source for information. You can buy them used on Amazon for not much money, skip to chapters that interest you, highlight, make notes, and reference them later in the future. I challenge you to read one book every week on a subject that moves you closer to realizing your PCC.

Shadowing a professional in a field that interests you is also a great way to learn about a career or field firsthand. Most people are more than willing to allow someone to shadow them in their careers and ask questions about their work.

As a senior in high school, I had an opportunity to shadow someone in the medical field. All seniors at my school had this type of opportunity: parents of other students in the school served as the professionals we shadowed.

Because I wanted to be a doctor, they paired me with a cardiologist. My day began at 7AM. I walked down a long windowless hallway to a door with only a name and a room number printed on a piece of plastic, screwed to the wall. An older gentleman in a white doctor's coat met me at the door. He introduced himself as Dr. Clark.

I walked into a small, cramped room. A window stretched the length of wall, from floor to ceiling, and offered only a sliver view of a crowded parking lot. There were several, teetering piles of paper stacked on his desk. He quickly ushered me in and pointed to a seat by his desk as he took a phone call. He picked up the phone, mid third ring, and abruptly brought the large black receiver to his ear. I could tell he was in a rush—and that he didn't particularly want to talk to the person on the other end.

I didn't catch most of the information, but it involved money and insurance companies. Not exactly inspirational topics for a young man who had a more ideal, if not naïve, belief that doctors only made sick people better.

Later in the day, I followed Dr. Clark into a surgery. I met the man who was about to have open-heart surgery, minutes before he was put under anesthesia. His eyes looked desperate and scared. Dr. Clark acknowledged this man's fear, but he only hesitated for a moment before calming the man in an abrupt, almost defiant, tone of confidence.

Before this day, I could only imagine what it might be like to be a doctor. Because of this experience, however, I had much greater context around what this job involved. I imagined myself in this role, years from now, and it didn't resonate with me. This experience helped open my mind to other opportunities and encouraged me to explore different career options that better suited my interests.

Take charge of your education. Read books on subjects that interest you, and get out into the world and have authentic experiences related to your interests and passions.

What are some ways you can teach yourself about your PCC?

1. _____

2. _____

3. _____

4. _____

5. _____

6. _____

7. _____

8. _____

3. THINK OUTSIDE THE JOB BOX

Although I encourage you to shadow and learn from others in their own careers, I want you to CREATE your own job. Your PCC will not be found in a job posting. You will not apply for your PCC. No one will train you into your PCC. You will be your own boss. The work you do now will create something that grows and gains momentum.

Instead of applying for a job, here are some other ideas:

1. Start a business.
2. Invent, produce, and sell a product.
3. Develop and license new technologies.
4. Create art, music, movies, or literature.
5. Help the environment, animals, or others that can't help themselves.
6. Teach others how you see the world.

When you become your own boss, you don't need to punch in on a time clock or do things for the benefit of someone else. Creating your own PCC gives you the FREEDOM to do the things you love. Imagine if you could go on vacation or spend time with family and friends and not have to worry about being to work on Monday morning or if you have enough money in your bank account.

It will take time, but eventually, your PCC will gain enough momentum that you can take breaks and step away for a day, a week, or even several months. After taking these breaks, you will come back to things that bring joy into your life with a renewed sense of enthusiasm and fresh passion.

4. DRESS WELL

I bought my first new two-piece suit the other day. I don't know how many times I will wear it, but when I need to look professional, it's in my closet. How you present yourself to the world is how the world will perceive you, and it's how you will perceive yourself as well.

Unfortunately, people do form a lot of their opinions about who we are based on how we look and dress. If we don't look nice, they assume we are lazy, not a professional, or just don't care.

If you want to exude success and competence, here are some tips:

Guys:

1. Wear an ironed shirt; I like heavy starch because it makes the shirt look and feel crisp.
2. Make sure your tie has a dimple in the middle and that it drops above or at your belt, but not below.
3. If your shirt has lines or a pattern, wear a solid tie.
4. Wear flat-front pants without the cuff at the pant bottom. The leg should have one or maybe two breaks in the material, but not more.
5. If you are wearing a blazer or suit coat, either don't use buttons, or only the top one or two, but never the third.

6. Jeans are ok if they are designer and not the baggy look. Wear a nice dress shirt or blazer; make sure to tuck in your shirt. Citizens for Humanity or Diesel are a couple of my favorite brands for jeans: the waist should be tight around the hip; they will stretch.
7. Don't underestimate the value of a nice belt with some character.

Girls:

1. A straight black pant leg is a nice, clean look.
2. Pencil skirts make you look instantly professional.
3. Make sure your clothes fit well so you will be confident and not spend all day tugging at your shirt.
4. If you are going to wear heels, make sure you can actually walk in them!
5. Don't be afraid to incorporate some color into your wardrobe!

In business and in life, we play roles. Dress for the role you want to play, and the curtain will open.

5. BE AUTHENTIC

Be honest with others, but more important, be honest with yourself. Just because your friends, family, or society tells you to do something doesn't mean it's right for you.

Be able to admit and accept this.

During my freshman year of college, I spent several hours a day composing music on a piano at a nearby dorm. The dorm where I lived had only a clunky upright in the basement, so I didn't like playing on this piano. Sometimes it would be late at night, and I wouldn't turn on any lights in the room. There was a street light not too far from the window, and it created enough glow in the room to see the keys. The piano was a grand, but I kept the lid down so it wouldn't make much noise and bother the residents.

At the time, it was my dream to compose music for an orchestra that I would conduct. I didn't want to be a traditional conductor with a boring conducting stick, however. I imagined twirling and throwing silk scarves in the air. I also didn't want to wear a boring tuxedo, but instead planned to wear colorful "rock-star"-inspired clothes. I made some of these clothes with an old Singer sewing machine, and I practiced my conducting routines in front of mirrors.

I remember walking down frat row one day on the way to a meeting at the U-Y: I was wearing tight, pink, leather pants. I'm surprised I didn't get beat up, and I definitely drew some attention. Looking back now, I cringe, but I'm proud of my courage to remain authentic.

6. BE ARTISTIC

Whatever your PCC becomes, you will need to communicate your ideas, product benefits, services, etc. Numbers, words, and data can tell only so much; an artistic and well-designed visual identity goes a long way. People will have more trust and interest in what you are doing if you tell your story in a straightforward, visually appealing way. Just as people judge how you dress, they will also judge how your PCC "dresses."

My moving truck has four-foot tall piano keys lining the box of the truck. When people see our truck on the road, they can easily see we are a piano-moving company. The keys engage our customers in a fun way that isn't "in your face." Customers like showing the giant keys to their kids. The keys sell our business in a fun and unique way.

When you need to explain an idea and inspire, nothing does a better job than a colorful, well-designed brochure, flyer, floor stand, or sign. Also, using photographs is a great way to explain your concept or vision. K44K has four programs related to our mission of *inspiring young people to believe in themselves through the arts and mentorship*. In order to explain our programs better, we created four floor banners that have pictures representing each program. Our designers made colorful designs around each of these pictures, fit the design into a template, and sent these to our printer. We use them at conventions, fairs, and festivals so people can immediately understand and appreciate what we do.

When I was at the U-Y, I used Microsoft Publisher to design brochures and flyers to recruit volunteers for MUSE. In the beginning, I recommend keeping your costs down by doing graphic design on your own computer. When you're first starting out, you may have several ideas that may change and evolve in a short amount of time. Eventually, I recommend hiring a professional to design your logos, marketing materials, and signage to ensure a quality product and clear message.

When I first started K44K, I put flyers in car windshields, front doors, and newspaper boxes. I printed posters and put them in windows of local businesses and the walls of community centers.

Placing marketing materials around your local community is free and a great way to tell others about your PCC. People love to support local causes, so let your colorful marketing materials inspire them!

7. DON'T BE AFRAID TO MAKE MISTAKES

In the beginning of my business, I made all kinds of mistakes. I remember trying to put new key tops on a piano for one of my first customers. The family had spent several months refinishing the outside of the piano and it looked beautiful.

I went to their house, took the keys out of the piano and brought them to my parents' house. I used a router and a jig to remove the old broken ivories and then glued new plastic ones to the keys and sanded and shaped the edges with a file. When I finished, the keys were crooked and looked horrible. The family was so nice and understanding, but I felt terrible.

When you are first getting started in your PCC, you will be on your own, learning as you go. You are going to make mistakes, but keep moving forward, you will get better!

8. SHOW UP AND BE EARLY

I promise my success has little to do with my abilities. There are many, many people who are more competent, hard-working, and talented than I am. However, I am successful because I show up.

This morning, I got up at 6 AM to work on an application to paint pianos at Mall of America (MOA) this spring. MOA allows nonprofits to use space there for events and fundraisers for free. It would be a great visibility opportunity for us, and it could potentially draw more people to the mall, so it's a win/win.

The events committee at MOA is probably meeting as I write this. They might say yes, they might say no, but the application is in, and I showed up.

And since you are going to show up, why not be early? Think how much you can accomplish if you are early! I woke up at 3AM the other day and couldn't get back to sleep, so I decided to start my day. I went to the health club, ran 2 miles, had breakfast, caught up on e-mails, and voted in the 2012 elections, all before 8am.

I completely crashed at around 4pm and had to take a nap, but it felt great to be ahead of the game. What could you accomplish if you got up an hour earlier every morning?

9. SEE POSSIBILITIES

In the last year of a three-year lease at my Minneapolis store, annual piano sales had gone down from $30,000 in 2007 to $20,000 in 2008. Some months, I sold only one piano, and I considered closing the store after the lease expired. I stayed positive, however, and believed I could still find a way to ensure the success of the business.

I knew I needed to make changes in my model, however, and I thought if I found a larger space, this might help. It would mean more investment and higher risk, but I felt additional space would allow for greater selection and hopefully increased sales.

Next door, a small storefront sat unoccupied with boards plastered to the windows. My store and this store had originally been one space, but the landlord had divided them into two units years ago. In order to combine the space again, all I would need to do was to knock down one small section of a wall.

The vacant room still smelled of curry and onion from the Indian grocery store that had previously occupied the space. When the store had been in business, I went there once in a while and bought a cold Coke on hot summer days.

The store used to have wire mesh shelves with outdated bottles of ketchup, mustard, and olives sprawled across the shelves. Much of the shelf space remained bare, and dusty loaves of bread stood watch over the empty landscape.

My landlord, Roger, encouraged me to expand and utilize this now-vacant space. Roger had been a construction worker for most of his life and had deep cracks in his leathery hands from years of mixing cement and sanding drywall. I felt he looked out for me like a father would, and he always seemed to be carrying a cement-soaked shovel or tool box around the property.

In addition to my concerns about limited space, however, I also worried that my poor sales might have something to do with the location. I initially moved into this space because of the cheap rent, but then I saw how it might be limiting the growth of my business.

Since I had been at this location, someone had been shot during a drug deal gone wrong directly across the street, and an employee of a convenient store located on the corner had also been shot on Christmas day. My customers were mostly families with young kids, and this neighborhood didn't feel safe or welcoming.

So in addition to exploring the space next door, I also went online and looked at other available warehouses in the area. I found a listing online for a large 6,000 sq/ft warehouse with "great light," located on Grand Avenue in St. Paul. That location offered my customers a much more family-friendly location, so I called the landlord in the listing and asked to see the property. He arranged for me to meet his property manager, Jack, later that day.

Jack met me at an upscale children's clothing store in front of the building. Several stores lined the building, and behind all of these stores sat the large warehouse space I came to see. Jack had a shaved head and broad, round shoulders. He had a lot of energy, and he eagerly shook my hand as he introduced himself.

We entered the upscale clothing store, walked past clothing racks protruding from the walls, opened a back door, and walked down a long, narrow hallway. Eventually the hallway opened into a large main room. Five commercial windows dotted the walls and yes, they created "great light." There had been an upholstery shop in this space previously, and cushions and foam lay scattered on the floor. Ceiling tiles sat haphazardly in metal frames, and the walls were pocked by dozens of holes. The smell of burned grease from a neighboring Chinese restaurant filled the air.

Even in its run-down state, I saw the potential of this location. I knew I had found the next home of K44K. I signed a lease and made the move with two cube vans running pianos back and forth across the city. The decision proved to be a good one, and I did more than $100,000 in sales during the first year in the new location.

I had been going back and forth about the idea of expanding my business to the grocery store next door for over a year. I remember calling my friend Steve and asking for his advice, and he had told me to "go for it!" At the time, it felt like a huge risk. My rent would be even higher and I would have some build-out expense.

Looking back now, I realize I needed to think BIGGER. Moving my business to St. Paul brought K44K to a whole new level. If I had stayed in Minneapolis, I'm sure I would never have expanded to Chicago or Kansas City, and I would not be writing this book.

Do you see the possibility and potential of your PCC? Are you thinking big enough?

Store location in South Minneapolis in 2008.

10. EXERCISE

It might go against common sense, but exercising actually gives you MORE energy. If you want more energy, alertness, and better overall health, exercise. I suppose I don't need to convince you that exercise has many positive benefits; it's finding motivation and time to do it that's the challenge.

One thing I learned about exercise a few years ago: you don't need to push yourself to the max for positive results. If you sustain your target heart-rate two or three times a week for twenty or thirty minutes, you will see positive results. Target heart rate varies based on your gender, age, and more directly, your resting heartbeat. Target heart-rate is about 50-85% of your maximum heart rate and can usually be achieved with a light jog.

I would recommend a heart-rate monitor to make sure you are reaching your target heart rate. Exceeding your target heart rate can do more harm than good and also makes your work out strenuous and less enjoyable and therefore less likely for you to do it regularly! Most heart-rate monitors wrap around your chest and give you a digital read-out on a wristband, and they typically cost less than $100.

Most local gyms offer group exercise programs like cycling, yoga, or high-energy group dance classes like Zumba. These types of group exercise programs help give structure and discipline to your exercise program. It also makes working out more fun, challenging, and socially engaging.

Working out will give you more energy and will also help reduce stress, improve your mood, and allow you to have greater enjoyment of your PCC!

11. NETWORK AND LEARN FROM OTHERS

Shortly after staring MUSE, I attended a networking dinner at a local golf club. Tables covered in white cotton cloth extended end to end in the middle of a large room. Large beams of dark brown timber spanned the room's girth, and other, smaller boards spiraled to the ceiling.

After dinner, I noticed a man with a long, thin frame hovering around the perimeter of the room as he gazed out a window. A series of windows ran along an entire length of the room. Dark storm clouds rolled across the late afternoon sky, and light drops of rain sprinkled the glass. He might have been wondering about the looming cold front or maybe the bunker placement on the 18th hole, but his thoughtful gaze suggested deeper, more contemplative thoughts.

When we met, he extended his long, slender hand to me and I felt his bones and tendons shift slightly as I shook his hand. He told me his name was David, and he asked me many questions about MUSE. He seemed genuinely interested and invited me to his office later in the week.

It took me only a few minutes to drive to his office. His building was on the U of M campus and only fifteen blocks from the U-Y. The floors in the building were made of wood, aged and stained from years of use. The floors creaked and groaned under my step and dipped in the middle. I peered around a doorway into a room that looked more like a living room than an office. A leather couch hugged the wall to my left, and colorful paintings and tapestry covered the surrounding walls.

David sat in a chair in the corner, reading a book, but he stood up to greet me with a warm smile and handshake. He wore a grey knit sweater, jeans, and moccasin slip-on shoes. We sat together over a cup of tea and discussed his passion for sailing. I told him I also shared this passion, and we discussed the sloop he had recently sailed and his dream to sail around the world.

A few minutes into our conversation, he told me he had good news: he had lined up an $8,500 grant for my newly-formed nonprofit. The funds were "restricted," which meant I had to use them for a specific purpose. In this case, I needed to use the funds to hire an organizational development consultant. David told me he had a person in mind, a woman named Suzanne. When he first told me about the funds being restricted, I didn't think I needed any help and that I had better ways to spend this money. I soon learned the benefit of Suzanne's expertise.

During my first meeting, Suzanne gave me a huge hug and told me how excited she was to be working with me. Tears welled up in her eyes as she told me about her passion to help nonprofits fulfill their missions. Suzanne had many years of experience in the nonprofit world, and she had become a consultant to share her vast knowledge.

At this time, I didn't have my own office, so our first official meeting occurred at a nearby restaurant. We sat at a table in the middle of the dining area and ordered coffee. I don't drink coffee, but I thought it would be nice to enjoy a cup with our conversation. I was a little over twenty years old at this time and talked a thousand words a minute, jumping from one thought to the next. Ideas flowed from my mouth like a faucet left running.

"Stop," she said.

She told me I rambled and talked too much. I listened to her and as a result, she taught me how to be concise and to the point. She made a list of specific talking points that I memorized. She told me to put all my other ideas in an imaginary box and set them aside for now because I would overwhelm people if I told them everything on my mind.

I listened and took her advice.

About a month later, we had our first official board meeting. The U-Y offered me a conference room, complete with a white board and swivel chairs. Because of the influence and instruction from Suzanne, I had an organized agenda and talking points for the meeting.

I had clear and concrete ideas to discuss, and I allowed time for others to share their thoughts.

There are people with experience and knowledge who can help and give you guidance. They may have already attempted something similar, or they may have knowledge in a specific area that you do not. Listen to them, work with them, and leverage their experience and expertise to reach your goals.

12. LOVE OTHERS

I don't believe we are individual, separate beings. I think we are like windows, shining light into a home we share, and we are more like the sunlight than the window.

Our minds might see separation in our physical forms, but our hearts understand a deeper, more permanent connection.

Helping others gives me the greatest reward and joy. I have seen the excitement in a child's eyes when she plays her piano for the first time. I have seen a woman come to tears because of the relief she felt when she found a home for her mother's treasured piano.

I assure you, find ways your PCC helps others, and you too will find unbounded joy.

Describe how your PCC could help others:

1. _____

2. _____

3. _____

4. _____

5. _____

6. _____

7. _____

8. _____

Kids playing a painted piano at the Loring Park Art Festival, 2012.

OCTAVE 3:

SET YOURSELF FREE

"THEY CAN BECAUSE THEY THINK THEY CAN."

-VIRGIL

1. MEDITATE

Quiet your mind.

Take ten minutes to sit still. You don't need to sit with your legs crossed or light any candles; just get yourself into a comfortable position. Dim the lights, and let your thoughts float across your mind like clouds in the sky. Don't fight or resist them; let them float away.

Listen and follow your natural breathing. Welcome the feeling of space and stillness.

By doing this, you will connect more fully with your fundamental self. Your fundamental self is free of attachment to material things and knows with absolute certainty the best and most direct path to your PCC.

If you can find time to meditate only once a week, that's ok. Make your goal to meditate three times a week for twenty minutes each time. I recommend the meditation book: *Quiet Mind: A Beginner's Guide to Meditation* by Sharon Salzberg.

2. LET GO

Life can be a stressful place, especially when you are charting your own creative career path. Many unpredictable bumps and turns come up along the way that can complicate things and cause frustration. Because we are human, we have an emotional response to this stress. This emotional response wastes energy and does not produce positive results. In fact, if you've ever slammed your fist or thrown something across a room, you know that an emotional response often makes things worse.

Thankfully, we can gain control over our emotions by releasing or letting them go. This helps us deal with our problems in a calm, collected, and rational manner.

I discovered a releasing technique called the Sedona Method several years ago. This technique was developed by a man named Hale Dwoskin and I highly recommend his book: *The Sedona Method: Your Key to Lasting Happiness, Success, Peace and Emotional Well-being.*

The Sedona Method teaches us that all humans have five basic wants:

1. Wanting Approval

2. Wanting Control

3. Wanting Safety

4. Wanting Oneness

5. Wanting Separateness

When we let go of WANTING these five basic human desires, we actually invite more of these things into our lives. It's the actual WANTING that gets in our way. For example, once we let go of wanting security, we can easily walk across a narrow beam high in the air. If we WANT security, we will be nervous, shaky, and more likely to fall.

Starting and running K44K has brought its fair share of stress. I remember the pressure and complications that came along with the expansion to Chicago. At the time, I didn't realize I needed a special license to move pianos in the state of Illinois. I received a call one afternoon from one of my movers saying the truck had been pulled over and towed to an impound lot. I spent the next few days trying to figure out how to get $500 in cash to one of my employees to get the truck out of the lot. Because this situation happened three hundred miles away, I had to let go of *wanting control.*

In order to let go of our emotions, we first have to welcome the feelings of stress or anxiety, instead of resisting them. Pay attention to where you physically feel them in your body, and "dive into" these sensations. Allow them to rest for a moment, and then ask which of the five basic wants— approval, control, safety, oneness and separateness—the stress is related to; it can be more than one of the wants. In the next step, ask yourself if you could let go of this want. Take a deep breath in, exhale, and allow the emotion to leave your body. Repeat until the emotion is washed away completely.

3. LET GO OF WANTING APPROVAL

I desperately wanted approval from my largest and most consistent donor: an investment firm in downtown Minneapolis.

The investment firm had only a handful of talented investors, and one of them saw a news story about me and invited me to their office around 2001.

I could hardly contain my excitement as I threw clothes out of my closet, searching for a pair of black slacks. I had prepared colorful folders, complete with pictures and descriptions about MUSE. On my way out the door, I cinched a tie around my neck and hoped the committee wouldn't notice my razor burn.

When I arrived downtown, I circled in and around the one-way streets until I arrived at a tall, glass building. I wound my way down the spiral belly of the business center's parking garage and then made my way to the elevator.

A pleasant receptionist with a thin wired microphone invited me to have a seat in the waiting area. I sat on a small couch near a table with a shiny vase perched on the surface.

Eventually, the receptionist brought me into a board room filled with executives. I told everyone seated in front of me about how I taught music and art to low-income youth at a local Boys & Girls Club. I told them about how we needed money for art supplies, staff salaries, and instruments. They all smiled with encouragement and told me they would have a meeting and let me know.

A few weeks after our meeting, I received a check in the mail for $5,000! It was the largest check I had ever held in my hand. I felt ecstatic and proud.

Every year, I would go back to this conference room, tell these executives about our program, and they would send me a bigger and bigger check. By the third year, they gave me a check for $25,000. I would write them thank-you cards, invite them to concerts, and frame artwork created by the kids as gifts.

After our program closed its doors in 2005, I felt I had let this investment firm down. For years, I felt like I needed to earn their approval and show them that their money had been well spent. Sometimes I would start letters to committee members I knew best, but I never knew what to say. I wanted to tell them I had done my best and that I felt so sad about having to close MUSE. I wanted to tell them I wouldn't give up and that I would rebuild the program.

All these emotions wasted valuable energy and distracted me from my current efforts. I started welcoming these feelings of wanting approval, dove into them, and eventually gave myself permission to let them go. I forgave myself and moved forward.

4. LET GO OF WANTING CONTROL

This sounds like a counter-intuitive thing for a business owner, but letting go of *wanting* control actually gives you *more* control. Again, the act of "wanting" gets in the way of being in the moment and making decisions without distractions.

We want things so we don't have to be afraid. I want money so I don't have to be afraid of starving or not having a place to sleep at night. I want success so I don't have to be afraid of being a failure, etc. Once we remove the fear, however, we exist in the moment. We can make decisions that are not clouded by fear that distracts from the present.

When I first expanded to Chicago, I worried people wouldn't want to buy or donate pianos. For a while, these questions paralyzed me in fear. I felt a cold blanket of fear envelop me when I thought about my recent expansion. Eventually, I learned to welcome these feelings, and I stirred up all my fear and anxiety until it felt like a tornado inside me. I then asked myself if I could let go of wanting control. I took a deep breath and said to myself, yes I can, and exhaled slowly.

Once I let go of wanting control, all these fears went away. I could make decisions that ensured that people DID donate pianos and DID buy them.

5. LET GO OF WANTING SAFETY

This world is chaotic and filled with things we can't control.

Accept it.

One day a man named Wally wandered into my store and asked me lots of questions about my business. Wally was a heavy-set, middle-aged man who could sight-read music better than anyone I know. When he smiled, he scrunched his face slightly, and he pushed his glasses back onto his face. After we talked further, he told me he wanted to volunteer at my store. I invited him back the next day to help out around the office.

Wally had been a general physician for most of his life, but a few years earlier, while he was stopped at an intersection, a cement truck had plowed into the back of his Volvo sedan. This accident caused a brain injury that affected his motor skills and short-term memory, and he could no longer practice medicine.

Wally proved to be a great asset for K44K. He helped write thank-you cards to our donors, take phone calls, and research the various pianos in our warehouse. He helped take some of the workload off my shoulders so I could focus on our recent expansion to Chicago.

Most of the time, I drove or took a plane when I traveled between the two cities, but Wally convinced me to take the train for one of these trips. I usually traveled alone, so I welcomed the company and the new experience.

Wally paid for the upgrade to a sleeper cabin on the train. We had our own room complete with a bathroom, table, and two beds. I took off my shoes, stretched my legs across the berth of the cabin and rested them on the adjacent couch. I pulled out my laptop and began working. I felt calm and at peace as our train glided through the Wisconsin countryside.

Wally and I talked casually about things we needed to accomplish on the trip and also made goals and set priorities for the coming year. Wally had a childlike wonder and excitement about the world. I didn't know him before his accident, but I suspect his brain damage made him see the world with more naiveté. I loved to talk with him about all the opportunities that existed in the world, and he shared my excitement: everything seemed possible.

While on the train, I took out my phone to check the balances of my bank accounts. I saw that my business account had less than $100 in it. I realized I must have forgotten about some withdrawals and felt the air in my lungs vanish. A wave of panic started in my feet and rolled through my body where it rested at the top of my head. A buzzing, popping feeling boiled on my forehead, and I felt too hot and quickly took off my zippered sweater.

I closed my eyes and dove into this fear that consumed my body. I asked myself if I could let go of wanting security. I took a deep breath in, said to myself, *yes I can*, and exhaled.

Calm and peace rushed back into my body as quickly as it had left. I wasn't worried. I knew we would sell pianos and get more money in our account. I gave myself permission, in that moment, to trust the universe.

By removing this fear, I gave myself the freedom to focus on things that I could control. I had the freedom to look at the world with clear vision and focused optimism.

6. LET GO OF WANTING ONENESS

Letting go of oneness means letting go of the feeling you need to fit in and belong. It's a common desire for people to want to be part of the group, to be like everyone else.

In college, I wanted to be like everyone else. I wanted to get good grades and earn a degree. I wanted to have a job and use my education. Unfortunately, I didn't know exactly what I wanted to do for my career, and I kept changing my major. I started as a pre-med major, then education, then nonprofit management, until I finally dropped out in my 3rd year.

Looking back now, I put too much emphasis on my actual major. Picking a major doesn't set your career path in stone, and it would have been easier for me if I had chosen a major that interested me and completed my degree.

I felt frustrated when I couldn't find a major that completely aligned with my interests. After I dropped out, I regretted not having a degree to hang on my wall. I felt like a failure for wasting so much time, money, and energy sitting through all those long lectures and mid-term exams. Several times, I debated going back and finishing, but I never found the motivation. I had a job I loved running the MUSE program, and I didn't see how having a degree would benefit me.

I still had this feeling, however, of wanting to be like everyone else. I wanted to be a college graduate. One day, I dove into this emotion of wanting to be like my friends and family who had college degrees. In addition to wanting to fit in, I also wanted love and approval from others. I wanted to know that people could accept me for dropping out of college.

I let all these emotions stir up inside of me. When I took a deep breath and let them go, I found the peace and acceptance I desperately needed. I understand we all must make decisions in our lives that make sense for US. Going to college didn't work for me, and I'm glad now I had the confidence to make this decision. When I let go of wanting oneness and approval from others, I found peace with this decision.

I hope you have the confidence to make decisions in your life that are right for YOU. You don't need to make the same decisions everyone else does in order to be accepted.

7. LET GO OF WANTING SEPARATENESS

Letting go of wanting separateness means letting go of the feeling you want to be independent or free from someone or something. We all crave our independence in some way or another and this emotional resistance can drain our energy and create distraction.

I remember when I was in high school, I didn't like to be part of a group. I refused to be in group photos, and I always sat in the back of the classroom. I didn't feel good enough to be included, and I also wanted to protect my independence.

Over the years, I have slowly let go of wanting separateness. I realize I have value and can freely share ideas and passion with others.

When I sit at board meetings for K44K, I want to be there. We all want to be at this table because we work together as a team. We have the same desire to inspire kids to believe in themselves, and as a group, we share our talents and energy to achieve this goal.

We exist as part of a greater community, and by working together, we help and care for one another.

8. BE OK WITH THE WORST-CASE SCENARIO

Doing new and different things can be scary. Sometimes we don't even know what we fear: we fear the unknown, and this paralyzes us from action.

So imagine your absolute worst-case scenario coming true. Maybe your worst-case scenario is running out of money and realizing you are completely broke. Maybe your greatest fear is realizing everyone thinks you are a failure. Maybe you spend a year of your life working towards a goal, yet accomplish nothing. Maybe you do find tremendous success and you're not sure you want this.

Whatever the worst-case, scariest scenario might be for you, describe it in detail below:

_____

_____

_____

_____

_____

_____

By defining your worst-case, scariest scenario, you take away its power. By confronting your fear on this sheet of paper, you look it directly in the eyes and free yourself.

If you have a scary monster in the closet, you turn on the light and the fear goes away. When you finally stand up to a bully and show him you are not afraid, you take away his power. So turn the light on in the closet, stand up to your bully, and remove all your fear.

9. EMBRACE CHAOS

Although it's important to be organized, embracing chaos helps you realize many opportunities, insights, and innovations. As you create your PCC, you will be reinventing your life, and there is no way to predict all the outcomes of your choices. Opportunity exists in this chaos, so be ready!

A couple of years ago, we asked an artist to come up with ideas for utilizing old piano parts. We gave her a pile of old piano wire, hammers, pedals, and piano keys. She came up with an idea for earrings and necklaces made out of piano hammers, a coat rack made out of piano pedals, and business card holders made out of piano keys. We didn't know what she would come up with, or if we could use any of her ideas, but she welcomed the chaos and found opportunity in a box of old piano parts. We now use her business-card-holder design for our staff at all of our locations, and we even sell them in our display cases and at this website: www.uncommongoods.com.

I also embrace chaos when I spend time with kids and listen to their ideas. When I taught MUSE, I asked the kids how I should teach them or run the program. They LOVED to tell me their ideas. Kids give their honest and uninhibited opinions, so you get some wild ideas.

When you are forming your PCC, allow space for new ideas and creativity to happen. Ask a seven-year-old what she thinks about your PCC.

10. PUSH YOUR COMFORT ZONE

It's not comfortable to do unfamiliar things and to push our comfort zone. When we do these things, however, we make discoveries about ourselves, find opportunities, and bring ourselves closer to realizing our PCC.

In order to make these discoveries and push our comfort zone, we need practice doing things not familiar to us.

Here are some ideas:

1. Make a ridiculous request from a stranger. Do this ten times.
2. Ask five strangers in public what their name is and give them yours.
3. Spend two days in complete isolation.
4. Cook something you've never made and invite your friends over for dinner.
5. Try different kinds of food. Maybe go to a sushi restaurant and try eel!
6. When you are in an elevator, instead of facing the door, face the people.
7. Say "Yes" to more things in your life. There is a great book called *Yes Man* by Danny Wallace.
8. Do public speaking with Toastmasters. This organization has many locations and opportunities around the country for people to go to events and get practice and gain skills in public speaking. www.toastmasters.org.
9. Try a new sport! Some examples: kite surfing, rock climbing, yoga, or paddleboard!

11. REMOVE YOUR EGO

Ego attaches itself to ideas and things. It might be a car or a home, a job title, or a bank account. None of these things represents the REAL you. Let your job be the fulfillment of your passions, let your vehicle be a tool that brings you to an important appointment, and let your house be the place where you nurture and raise your family.

There's nothing wrong with having and enjoying nice things, but don't let them DEFINE you.

After I lost funding and had to close MUSE, I felt a deep, personal loss. I had identified with running this program, and I felt like a part of me had died when it ended. I became so entangled with the business that I lost sight of where my identity ended and the business began.

I now realize that working for K44K perfectly aligns with my own passions and interests, but the business itself is NOT me. I no longer feel personally connected, but instead, I have a feeling of tremendous gratitude and appreciation that I get to do something I love every day. This separation helps me be a better boss for my employees and a better leader for the organization.

12. KNOW THAT THE OPPOSITE OF FEAR IS LOVE

When you get stuck or feel hopeless, invite love into your life. Your mind will find and create fear, and these thoughts can run circles around you until you trap yourself in a prison of fear. The only thing that can break these shackles of fear is love. I wrote a poem years ago that helped me remove fear from my life. I don't remember most of it now, except for the last line:

THERE IS LOVE ALL AROUND US, WHEN QUIET ENOUGH AND STILL ENOUGH, TO SEE

I often repeated this line to myself, and it helped me stay grounded in a place of love. There cannot be fear where there is love, and there can be no darkness where there is light.

Ice Breaker Event at Mall of America, 2013.

OCTAVE 4:

FIRST STEPS

"THE FUTURE BELONGS TO THOSE WHO BELIEVE IN THE BEAUTY OF THEIR DREAMS."

-ELEANOR ROOSEVELT

1. DEFINE WHY

Can you define what EXACTLY draws you to your PCC? Can you boil this idea down into one defining sentence that answers the question: WHY did you choose this PCC?

I remember reading a book when I first started MUSE that had this quote by Martin Luther King Jr.:

> *"BEFORE YOU TEACH A CHILD TO READ OR WRITE, FIRST TEACH THEM TO BELIEVE IN THEMSELF."*

When I read this, I knew, THAT WAS IT! This idea defined and focused my work from that day forward. When I taught kids to play piano, I taught them to believe in themselves. When I moved a piano, I earned money for MUSE, a program that taught kids their importance and value.

I recently saw a presentation by a person named Simon Sinek. Simon talked about how great companies and great leaders answer the *why* question first, then the *how*, and then the *what*. In contrast, uninspired leaders answer the *what*, then the *how*, and finally the *why*.

For example, salespeople at an uninspired piano store will tell you they have quality, warranted pianos at competitive prices (the *what*). They will tell you they import pianos from Asia in large containers in order to keep the cost down for you the customer (the *how*). They would then ask if you would like to buy a piano (the *why*).

In contrast, K44K addresses the *why* question first. K44K inspires young people to believe in themselves (the *why*). We do this by supporting four arts and mentorship-based programs in local communities (the *how*). Oh, and we raise money for this by selling donated pianos; would you like to buy one? (The *what*.)

Simon talked about how humans make decisions using the part of our brain that answers the *why* question, the part connected to our emotions. We then justify our decision using the rational part of our brains that focus on the *what* and *how* questions.

If you want to find success in your PCC, make sure you answer the WHY question FIRST.

Define the WHY for your PCC:

_____

_____

_____

_____

_____

2. THINK LIKE AN ENTREPRENEUR

It's time to get the creative juices flowing. Pull out the whiteboard. Throw balls against the wall. Turn up the music. Take a bath. Go for a drive.

When do you feel most creative? When do you feel your thoughts flowing? DO THAT.

Think of ways you can incorporate your passion into some type of product or service that can benefit others.

When you turn your passions into a career, you need to think like an entrepreneur. An entrepreneur finds creative solutions to problems and makes a profit from these solutions. Finding a solution to problems that benefits others and makes a profit will be essential to a successful PCC. So what problems can you solve? How can you capitalize on these opportunities?

The fact that K44K sells used pianos offers nothing new to the marketplace: stores have sold used pianos for a long time. Although unique, the charity aspect does not by itself ensure our success.

The problem that we solved—and in my opinion, the central reason for our success—is this: we found a solution for unused, old pianos sitting in people's homes. People can't easily store a piano in a closet or throw it away in a trash can, or even give it away to a neighbor. We provide piano owners with the option to donate their old pianos, have them moved by a professional moving company, and on top of this, receive a tax-deductible receipt. By providing a simple solution for their unused pianos, we have created a virtually endless supply of pianos.

Problems and their creative solutions exist EVERYWHERE. Solve a problem related to your PCC, and success will follow.

Think of some problems:

_____

_____

_____

_____

_____

_____

Now list some solutions to those problems:

_____

_____

_____

_____

_____

_____

_____

3. BE CREATIVE AND REDUCE COMPETITION

If you want to be a doctor or teacher, prepare yourself for a lot of competition. Many talented, hard-working people want to be doctors or teachers. In fact, most jobs in the marketplace remain extremely competitive, especially in our current economic climate.

Separate yourself. Do something different.

CREATE your dream job.

Instead of becoming a "traditional" teacher, I started MUSE. By doing this, I experienced many benefits. Because I taught after school, I didn't have the same restrictions on lesson material and curriculum topics that are dictated by the board of education. I had the freedom to focus on a curriculum that improved kids' self-esteem and helped make them feel good about themselves. By creating my own job, I specialized in the things that inspired me to teach in the first place.

How can you create a job that gives you the freedom to focus on your OWN passions? It will take some ingenuity, but believe me, creating your own path will make the entire process easier and more rewarding in the long run. Because you design it, it will also be specific and customized to your own unique passions.

4. BE WILLING TO SOUND CRAZY

Be willing to tell people about your goals and plans, but be careful who you tell. Some people will discredit you and bring you down if your goals seem too difficult or implausible to them. Sometimes, people want to discourage you because they think this protects you, and they have their best intentions at heart. Other people are jealous. You don't want to tell your dreams to either of these kinds of people; they will steal your energy and momentum.

At our last board meeting, I told the board about my plan to expand K44K to fifty cities in the next ten years. I know we can't do it overnight, and it does sound crazy, but I want them to know my vision. I want the world to know my vision. When I'm ninety years old, I want to look back at my life and feel like I left nothing on the table.

What are you afraid to leave on the table?

_____

_____

_____

_____

_____

5. MAKE TODAY THE FIRST DAY OF THE REST OF YOUR LIFE

I worked as a blackjack dealer for about four years after I turned eighteen. Every forty minutes of dealing cards, I had a twenty-minute break. While on break, most dealers played cards or smoked. To me, however, doing anything with cards on my break made no sense, and I didn't smoke.

So I spent most of my breaks reading books or writing in my notebook. I made drawings of ideas or wrote goals and timelines for my life. I felt my job limited the time I could devote to my goals, but I had to make my car and mortgage payments each month. For months, I considered putting in my two weeks notice, but fear kept me from doing it.

After all, I had a pretty good life, and my steady paycheck afforded me nice things. I felt, however, that I would miss many experiences and adventures if I continued to work as a blackjack dealer.

Eventually, I gave my two weeks notice and, on my last day, shared a chocolate cake with fellow employees. They hugged me and wished me good luck.

My art teacher in college told me some artists fear a blank canvas. A blank canvas represents unlimited possibility, but it also overwhelms us: we don't know where to begin. The day I left my blackjack job, I had a blank canvas in my life, and I can still feel the fear and excitement that mixed together like paint on a palette.

When I quit my job, I created the space and time I needed to create my PCC. I didn't know exactly what it would look like, but I picked up a brush and started painting.

It was the first day of the rest of my life.

6. SET GOALS

Now that you have determined what things bring you JOY, have defined your passion, and have some ideas about how to turn these passions into a career, let's set some goals! They should be achievable, specific, and they should get you EXCITED!

Big goals can be overwhelming, so it might help to break them down into smaller ones.

Goal #1:   Completed by: _____

_____

_____

_____

_____

_____

Goal #2:   Completed by: _____

_____

_____

_____

_____

_____

Goal #3:   Completed by: _____

_____

_____

_____

_____

_____

Goal #4:   Completed by: _____

_____

_____

_____

_____

_____

_____

Draw a picture of your most exciting goal.

Now make a list of things you need to do in order to achieve this goal:

1. _____

2. _____

3. _____

4. _____

5. _____

6. _____

7. _____

8. _____

Can you do any of these things today? Go through this process for all your goals.

Get started!

7. TAKE ACTION

This point in the process becomes a sticking point for people. Why is it so difficult to take that first step? It might be a phone call or a meeting with someone from the community, but you have reached the point where your idea, the goal you want to achieve, can no longer exist only in your imagination.

In order to achieve success, you will need to take action in the real world.

There might be risks or sacrifices to consider and 1,000 reasons to not take action.

Do it anyway.

I want to share some words of inspiration and wisdom with you. Quotations like these have been a great source of clarity and guidance in my life. I hope they help you gain traction in achieving your goals and help provide motivation to start your PCC.

"FORTUNE SIDES WITH HE WHO DARES."

-VIRGIL

"WHAT LIES BEHIND US AND WHAT LIES BEFORE US ARE TINY MATTERS COMPARED TO WHAT LIES WITHIN US."

- RALPH WALDO EMERSON

"WHENEVER YOU FIND THE WHOLE WORLD AGAINST YOU, JUST TURN AROUND AND LEAD THE WAY."

- ANONYMOUS

"THE BEST WAY TO PREDICT THE FUTURE IS TO CREATE IT."

- UNKNOWN

"THERE ARE ONLY TWO RULES FOR BEING SUCCESSFUL. ONE, FIGURE OUT EXACTLY WHAT YOU WANT TO DO, AND TWO, DO IT."

- MARIO CUOMO,
GOVERNOR OF NEW YORK

"SOONER OR LATER, THOSE WHO WIN ARE THOSE WHO THINK THEY CAN."

- RICHARD BACH, BEST-SELLING AUTHOR
OF JONATHAN LIVINGSTON SEAGULL

"WHAT YOU DO SPEAKS SO LOUDLY THAT I CANNOT HEAR WHAT YOU SAY."

- RALPH WALDO EMERSON

"TO AVOID CRITICISM DO NOTHING, SAY NOTHING, BE NOTHING."

- ELBERT HUBBARD, AMERICAN WRITER
AND PHILOSOPHER

"HE WHO HAS A WHY TO LIVE CAN BEAR ALMOST ANY HOW."

- FRIEDRICH NIETZSCHE,
GERMAN PHILOSOPHER

8. PACE YOURSELF

For a couple of months last summer, I moved pianos with Jack, our main St. Paul mover. Jack has moved pianos for me for the last three years, and he rarely misses a day. I looked forward to learning moving skills and getting to know him better while we drove between jobs.

During the first few days of working together, I thought Jack was being lazy. When we pulled up to a house, he wanted to back up the truck and lower the ramp onto the front sidewalk or porch in order to avoid lifting the piano over a few steps. Several times, I said to him, "Jack, let's carry it."

"Ooooh, no," he said in a sure and confident tone. And so instead, we used the ramp.

By the end of the week, I started to understand. When you're moving eight or more pianos each day, as well as driving 500+ miles in a cube van, every little amount of effort starts to make a difference. I remember driving to a job on the last day of a long week: it was about forty miles northwest of the Twin Cities. The late afternoon sun shone directly into our eyes as we fought rush-hour traffic, and I was exhausted. I realized Jack had been right: I should have been pacing myself more on those Tuesday moves.

Another hard-working employee, Andrew, fixes and tunes pianos at our St. Paul store. Andrew began his career in London and has fixed and tuned pianos for more than twenty-five years. Andrew is slow and meticulous: he stays until the job is done, and he makes sure the pianos are ready when they leave the store. Andrew works extra late on Fridays, sometimes until 9PM, so pianos are tuned and ready for our Saturday open house.

It's a fact that water, if given enough time, will wear away stone. Steady, reliable, and consistent work built my business, one front door step and one piano string at a time. When you start your PCC, don't feel you need to tackle a huge project, or dive headfirst into anything. Complete small tasks, and do these consistently.

What are some small tasks you can start doing now?

1. _____

2. _____

3. _____

4. _____

5. _____

6. _____

7. _____

8. _____

9. KNOW THAT IT'S OK TO STOP OR CHANGE DIRECTION

When I invested in real estate, I spent countless hours poring over houses listed for sale. For an entire year, I researched properties, examined title records, and narrowed down more than 10,000 potential properties to only two or three deals.

On separate occasions, I misfiled paperwork with the county and lost opportunities to purchase properties. These deals represented so much hard work and potential income. They slipped through my fingers because of silly mistakes I should not have made.

These mistakes resulted in one of the lowest points in my life. I made the difficult decision to stop investing in real estate full time. Because I made this decision, I created the opportunity to spend more time working for K44K. This helped me grow my business and create a successful PCC.

I still face many challenges, but I enjoy my work and it brings much greater joy and sense of reward to my life. I am glad I stopped doing something that didn't work for me and changed career paths. When you realize something is not working for you, don't be afraid to stop and change direction.

You have all the freedom in the world.

10. WHAT WILL YOU DO WITH THIS FREEDOM? COLLABORATE

Sometimes it's easier to get started if you collaborate with another person or organization that aligns well with your PCC. Maybe the other person or organization has the resources, and you can bring the skill set and passion? Maybe you have an idea about how to improve a product or service of another business? Maybe your product, service, or skill could complement something already in the marketplace?

Collecting pianos from the public began as a slow process. I received one or two pianos every week, but I wanted more! I called a few piano moving companies and asked them if they had any old pianos they no longer needed. A couple of them said they did and one even brought me around twenty pianos. Before I knew it, I was in business! Not only did this arrangement kick-start my business, it also helped these moving companies clear out some of their warehouse space. It was a win-win situation for everyone.

11. HAVE A CLEAR VISION

When you work long hours, experience unforeseen challenges, or want to give up, what will keep you going? For me, it has always been a clear vision of what and why I am working towards a particular goal. Vision should be felt, seen, and experienced in your mind, as if it were reality.

A clear and specific vision has the power to motivate and guide your progress. Sometimes, visions take years or even decades to accomplish. I have a clear vision of K44K existing in fifty cities around the country. I can picture the airplane I fly when I land at airports in these various cities and can hear the commotion of workers in our main office as we manage phone calls and e-mails from around the country.

K44K currently has locations in Chicago and Kansas City, but without this grand vision, I wouldn't have left St. Paul—or even left my parents' basement, for that matter!

Can you imagine a vision for your future? How does this vision make you feel?

Protect it.

It WILL become real.

12. BE YOUR VISION

I remember having lunch with Gregg, one of my board members and personal mentors, at the lake where he worked. Gregg supervised the lifeguards and maintained the grounds and had worked there every summer for the past twenty-five years.

A large patio extended from a hill that gradually sloped into the shore of the lake. Several large oak trees poked through the deck of the patio and created scattered patches of shade. We sat on a bench that, at least for the time being, found itself on an island of shade. Wind bursts chopped at the wave crests as I told Gregg about my frustration with the education system.

I told him about the number of tests my students had to take throughout the school day and how poorly they performed on these tests. I told him about how these low scores reinforced the notion of failure and hopelessness among the kids.

When I taught the same kids art and music, they lit up with excitement and pride. I didn't grade or judge them, and I believe this positive, reinforcing instruction brought out more of their potential than any test or grade ever could.

Gregg and I talked for several hours. Gregg loved analogies, so we imagined my ideal teaching environment as a place. We picked a random city, Rome, to function as this ideal teaching environment. He asked me to describe what Rome would be like to someone visiting for the first time. I told Gregg about how Rome would be a place that encouraged creativity and kids' natural desire to learn. Rome would awaken the potential that already exists within their students and help them be better than they thought they could be.

Gregg taught me that instead of trying to change other cities into Rome, I should instead BE Rome. At the time, this made so much sense. I didn't have to waste energy fighting the status quo, or changing people's minds, I only needed to create something that made sense to me. As Mahatma Gandhi once said, "be the change you wish to see in the world." I still remember the peace and calm I felt when I realized this truth.

Mall of America, Ice Breaker Event, 2013.

OCTAVE 5:
THE MOTIONS

"NOTHING WILL EVER BE ATTEMPTED IF ALL POSSIBLE OBJECTIONS MUST FIRST BE OVERCOME."

-SAMUEL JOHNSON

1. THINK BIG, START SMALL

A lot of people think they need to take out a big loan and risk everything in order to pursue their PCC. I started K44K as a full-time student and learned how to fix and sell pianos in my free time. I didn't take out loans; instead, I invested a nominal amount in tools and books, and I taught myself.

Instead of hiring a piano mover, I borrowed a friend's motorcycle trailer to move the pianos and sold them out of my parents' garage. Instead of hiring a graphic designer, I drew a picture of a piano and put my phone number underneath it. I then made copies of this image and put it on car windshields and on the handles of people's front doors.

Over time, I generated enough income to pay for an actual storefront and to hire professional designers to create a website and marketing materials.

Find creative solutions to start your PCC without taking out loans and minimize your risk.

2. DON'T BE LIKE THE MOST

Most piano stores don't tell kids to paint their pianos. Most pianos stores don't put twenty of their pianos in parks and on sidewalks for two months in the summer. Most piano stores don't give 100% of their profits to charity. Most piano stores don't turn their pianos into displays for brochures and posters. Most piano stores don't make business card holders out of old piano keys. Most piano stores don't encourage movies and music videos to be filmed in their stores. Most piano stores don't give away sheet music for free.

K44K is not like MOST piano stores.

When you create your PCC, separate yourself from the crowd and leave an impression. You want people to tell their friends, family, and co-workers about their experience with your PCC. This word of mouth "buzz" marketing will grow your PCC faster and more effectively than any "traditional" marketing campaigns.

Describe how your PCC will not be like the MOST:

1. _____

2. _____

3. _____

4. _____

5. _____

6. _____

7. _____

8. _____

Julie painting a piano at the Uptown Art Fair in 2010.

3. HAVE A SUSTAINABLE PLAN

Along with using profits from my piano sales to support MUSE, I also received several large grants and individual donations each year.

I started to rely on these grants and donations to help pay for art supplies, staff, and instruments. After a few years, key donors did not renew funding, and our program doors closed.

Although it worked for the initial years, depending on a few major grant renewals and donations proved unsustainable. Although many nonprofits do depend on grant and donation renewals each year, reliance on only a handful of grantors can be a recipe for disaster.

When you start your PCC, make sure you can sustain it: not for one or two years, but for the long term.

4. PROVE THE MODEL

I mentioned earlier that when I composed music on the piano, I dreamt of conducting my music in front of an orchestra, but instead of using a thin, traditional baton to keep rhythm, I planned to wave colorful silk scarves through the air. The scarves tapered at one end in order for them to create a fluid motion as they floated through the air. I felt the graceful arcing and circling of the scarves best represented the emotion of music. I had plans to put bean-bag weights in some of the scarves so I could throw them high into the air, and I also had sketches of silk parachutes that would float down into the audience.

Someone from the U-Y invented a made up word "chondrel" as a name for these scarves, and the name stuck. I also did an art project using chondrels in the MUSE program. I didn't use real silk with the kids but instead used cotton sheets that I cut and tapered with a scissors. We did a project that had kids tie-die them and wear them during the end of year concert. The kids loved to unravel their chondrels after dipping them into various buckets of color, and they loved showing off their colorful creations for family and friends.

Students in MUSE performing at the end of the year event in 2003.

I also came up with the idea to sell chondrels in gift shops in order to raise awareness and revenue for the MUSE program. I began buying silk in bulk from China and used a special kind of sewing machine to sew the edges. I made the scarves colorful and fun by using various colors of dyes and ink. I also hired a designer to come up with a cardboard tab used to hold the chondrels so they could hang from store display racks.

I had so much confidence these chondrels would *fly* off shelves, I ended up making more than 1,000 chondrels. I spent countless hours measuring, sewing, and decorating these creations. Eventually, I made a display rack out of wood and began approaching gift shops about this new and exciting product.

Although I did find a couple hospital gift shops to carry the product, it became more trouble than it was worth to keep the display replenished. I tried to sell them online as well, but I didn't have much luck.

In the end, I learned a valuable lesson. Instead of spending so many hours sewing and making these scarves, I should have made only a handful and tested the market on a smaller scale. The scarves worked well as an art project for the kids, and also as gifts to donors, but the large-scale, commercial distribution never became a reality.

Before you get too invested in time and resources, make sure you first prove your model.

5. REUSE

Why manufacture something if you can reuse something else? By reusing things, we help the environment by reducing waste created from the manufacturing process. This waste includes the energy needed to transport raw materials, to power machines, and to dispose of the excess, unused material. Reusing things can also be a big money saver because the supplier does not have to recoup a manufacturing cost.

At the turn of the century, there were more than 250,000 pianos sold each year in the United States. At that time, households didn't have computers or flat-screen TVs; the piano WAS the entertainment center. Owning a piano meant you had a real home.

A large percentage of these pianos still work and sit unused in homes across America. Producing pianos from raw materials today is extremely competitive and difficult. Pianos have more than 10,000 moving parts, and the labor and materials needed to assemble these instruments make profit margins incredibly thin.

Also, pianos made today are either very expensive or cheaply made in Asian markets; the middle ground is disappearing. By selling quality used pianos, I give the public an option to buy a good piano for not very much money.

Describe what used things *you* could leverage to make your PCC possible:

1. _____

2. _____

3. _____

4. _____

5. _____

6. _____

7. _____

8. _____

6. FLY THE PLANE

A few years ago, I decided I would learn how to fly airplanes. At first the idea scared me, but I wanted to challenge myself and do something adventurous.

I drove to a small airport in Crystal, Minnesota and scheduled my first lesson. My instructor, Mark, was in his mid-twenties, but his freckles and wrinkled skin made him look at least thirty. He had short, curly brown hair, lots of energy, and even more patience. I once tried to teach someone how to parallel-park, but after a few unsuccessful attempts, I couldn't do it anymore. I can't believe how someone could have the patience to teach people how to fly airplanes.

We stepped out onto a tarmac shared by about five metal birds, all resting in a neat row. I could hear the loud hornet buzz of an airplane powering up for takeoff. Jet fumes mixed with the vapors of hot asphalt steaming in the afternoon sun. The planes on the pavement in front of us had swooping propellers and metal riveted skin. Mark brought me to a Piper Warrior with the tail number N136PU. The plane had been built in the 1980s, and it still had the original orange upholstered seats.

The plane was a bottom wing, which meant the wings were below the cockpit. Mark pulled a lever on the door, and the door swung around and banged on the fuselage of the maroon striped plane. I stepped on to a part of the wing that had a rough, sandpaper material glued to it for traction. I lowered my 6'4" frame into a cramped, lever-and-gauge-filled cockpit.

During my first few lessons, Mark taught me a valuable lesson: *fly the plane*. This sounds obvious, but in emergencies, new pilots often get so focused on trying to restart a stalled engine or go through an emergency checklist that they forget their most important task: *no matter what, fly the plane.*

In my business, I need to stay focused on fixing, selling, and moving pianos. These activities keep my business in the air. These activities pay our bills and are what some people call "the bread and butter." Developing glossy marketing materials and choosing the right font on our website can become distractions to our essential business activities. These details are important, but the priority must always be on the customer who walked through the door, the piano that needs a sales tag, or the Craigslist ad that needs updating.

Describe the most essential functions of your PCC:

1. _____

2. _____

3. _____

4. _____

5. _____

6. _____

7. _____

8. _____

Me doing a pre-flight check on a DA-40 in 2011.

7. IF YOU WANT SOMETHING, ASK

How will the world know what you want if you don't ask? What's the worst thing that could happen? Oh yeah, someone could say "No." I don't think anyone has died from hearing this word, so go for it!

When I went to the U-Y, I had to ask if I could start an after-school program that taught music and art. They said YES. The U-Y gave me a cubicle and around twenty volunteers to help run my program. Pretty soon, my program taught more than 120 students each year at three different schools in North Minneapolis.

When I first started accepting pianos, I would only accept the pianos I could fix and sell for at least $500. I didn't like taking the large uprights because I usually couldn't get much money for them, and would sometimes lose money after I paid for the piano to be moved and fixed. One day, when I drove to pick up a large upright that LOOKED nice on the outside, I found out when I got there that the piano had major problems.

I told the donor we couldn't take the piano. I explained to her that I would lose money if we took pianos in this poor condition. Because I could see her strong desire to donate her piano, I came up with the idea to ASK her if she would be willing to pay $100 in order to help cover the cost to move and fix her piano. She said no.

But about two weeks later, she called me back to say she had changed her mind and had $100 ready for me.

From this day forward, I began ASKING people to pay money to help cover the moving expense for the less-expensive piano donations; this allowed me to accept any and all pianos. People appreciate having options, and this new policy both created options for the donor, as well as less-expensive options for my customers.

I only had to ASK.

8. STAY FOCUSED

When you design a job for yourself that aligns with your passions, you must be creative. I promise this will be a rewarding, exciting, and fun process!

Once the faucet of creativity gets turned on, however, be careful not to get distracted with every fantastic idea that pops into your head. These ideas can easily grow into side projects that consume your time and energy. In the beginning, all of your creative energy needs to be focused on establishing your PCC.

A few years ago, I looked on Craigslist for a used car. While searching through the listings, I found a school bus for $1,000. Suddenly I found myself daydreaming about what it would be like to turn this bus into a party on wheels. Instead of focusing on my piano business, I bought the bus and started installing sound systems and disco lights. I named the business, "A+ Party Bus," and drove around bachelor parties and birthday parties on the weekends for about two years.

I ended up making a little bit of money, but eventually, I realized the party-bus business did not align with my PCC. I ended up selling the company.

I could have saved a lot of time and energy by never starting this business, and instead invested myself more fully into K44K.

9. SET SMALL GOALS AND REWARD YOURSELF

Are you overwhelmed by a big project, don't know where to begin, or have trouble staying motivated?

Set small goals and reward yourself along the way.

I made a deal with myself while writing this book. If I would write for one hour in the morning at Perkins, I would treat myself to coffee and breakfast. I did the math, and this book cost me around $1,000 in omelets, coffee, and pancakes. This arrangement gave me the structure and motivation I needed to finish a large and challenging project. As a result, I now have something I can be proud of and hopefully use to inspire others.

Think about what you can accomplish if you set small goals and reward yourself along the way:

I will work for _____ hours doing the following:

_____

_____

_____

_____

In exchange for working _____ hours, I will reward myself by:

_____

_____

_____

_____

10. TEAM UP

Two young ladies came into my St. Paul store looking for a piano last year. Carla, who had dark hair and glasses, carefully examined various pianos and their prices as she strolled through the showroom floor. Maggie had blond hair tied above her head and stood near the entranceway with me, scanning the room and its labyrinth of pianos. I asked her about the purpose for the piano, and she began expressively waving her hands, like a conductor of an orchestra, as she described a music studio she and Carla hoped to start.

I could tell these young women possessed a lot of passion and excitement for their business as they told me about the studio layout and program curriculum they hoped to create. Did I detect a PCC?

I helped them find an inexpensive grand piano for around $1,000 and wished them good luck on their new business venture.

A few months later, Carla and Maggie invited me to coffee to discuss topics related to their business. They had some questions about turning the business into a nonprofit, and they wanted to hear about my experience applying for tax-exempt status from the IRS. Of course I obliged: after all, this directly involved a PCC!

While talking to them, I realized how well this partnership complemented their business. Carla had a keen sense of the numbers and details, while Maggie used her creativity to bring color and interest to the program curriculum and marketing materials. The two partners both respected the opinions and ideas of one another and truly worked as a team.

Do you know someone who shares your same passions and interests? Maybe you share skills and talents that would complement one another?

Make a list of people who might make a good partner:

1. _____

2. _____

3. _____

4. _____

11. SIMPLIFY

Einstein once said, *"Everything should be made as simple as possible, but not simpler."*

In art school, I remember my teacher once asking me, what I could take AWAY from the painting. I like this because most of the time, we would ask what needs to be ADDED.

In my office, when something is on my desk that I don't immediately need, I put it in a piano bench. (I use piano benches like drawers because we have glass desks and lots of benches.)

Removing extraneous non-important things in your life will help you focus on things that ARE important. Simplifying your life will focus your energy and help you excel.

Whether it is your calendar, business plan, inventory, or office space, ask yourself, "How can I simplify?"

12. KEEP MOVING

Earlier in my book, I wrote about how it's ok to stop or change direction in your PCC. Sometimes, you need to keep moving and get through difficult times. After I lost my funding and the board dissolved in 2004, I had a meeting with my consultant Suzanne. At the time, I didn't have any money, and she agreed to help me for free.

I remember sitting down with her at a round table in a back room of her office. A large tablet of paper leaned against an easel in the corner of the room, and only a dim light filtered through a window facing a waiting room. Everyone in her office had already left for the day and we shared a long quiet moment together. Suzanne asked me in a caring and thoughtful tone if I would like to dissolve the business. She told me I had no obligation to continue if I didn't want to.

At the time, I didn't have a clear vision or direction for the organization. I didn't know if I wanted to continue with MUSE, and if so, how I would secure funding. I still felt passionate about the mission to inspire kids to believe in themselves, but I didn't know how I wanted to do it.

I told her that I did NOT want to dissolve, and that I wanted to keep the organization alive. I made the decision to keep moving.

Sometimes you must put one foot in front of the other even if you don't know where these steps will take you. Movement by itself will create new opportunities and new inspiration.

It will come to you.

Piano painted by kids through the Paint a Piano program.

OCTAVE 6:
THE PRACTICAL

"STORMS MAKE OAKS TAKE ROOTS."

– PROVERB

1. PRODUCT SHOUT OUT

The following are products and services I highly recommend. These products and services have helped me run my business smoothly and effectively.

GOOGLE CALENDAR

At the beginning of the year, I create reminders on my Google calendar for employee birthdays, tax filing due dates, goal deadlines, truck maintenance reminders, etc. I also keep track of my own daily appointments, as well as the appointments for my piano movers and technicians. For example, we have a calendar for piano movers in Chicago and a calendar for piano technicians in Kansas City. I can view one or all of these calendars at the same time, and even access them from my smart phone.

LENOVO LAPTOP

A good friend who owns a computer repair shop recommended the brand Lenovo: he told me this brand is the industry standard for laptops. I took his advice and have been very happy with my Lenovo. For around $1,000, you can own one of these laptops and take your work on the road in confidence. I recommend getting the extended battery pack: it gives battery life for up to nine hours. You will also want some kind of computer bag to protect it.

OVERSTOCK.COM

I have had luck ordering dress shirts on overstock.com. I can usually find shirts for around $20 that would be more than $50 in a department store. Amazon.com doesn't have the same selection of shirts, so I recommend visiting this site if you can't find what you are looking for at Amazon.com.

AIRBNB.COM

When I travel now, I no longer stay in expensive, sterile hotels. People post their bedrooms, apartments, condos and even RVs on airbnb.com and rent them out by the day, week, or month.

When I visit Chicago on business, I save more than half the cost of a hotel. The stay feels more like I'm visiting a friend than traveling for business. Airbnb.com has listings all over the world, so the next time you travel, visit airbnb.com first!

CRAIGSLIST.ORG

I have used craigslist.org to advertise and sell pianos for years. It's free advertising and a great way to reach the general public. Craigslist continually improves its site. For instance, it recently improved the way pictures are posted and viewed.

Craigslist is also a great place to buy things. People post their used items on the site for much less money than you would pay in a store. It takes more effort to call the seller, make an appointment, and drive to their home, but for large purchases, it's worth it!

KICKSTARTER

I talk more about this later in the book, but Kickstarter. com is a website where you can share your ideas for a PCC and ask the public for financial support. In exchange for this support, you provide them with small products or gifts related to your product. You will share your idea by posting a short video about your PCC online. Share your excitement and creativity with the world and watch the dollars and support flood your inbox.

TED TALKS

Tedtalks.com shares short speeches and talks from industry leaders, visionaries, entrepreneurs, or otherwise interesting people. The website organizes the talks into various topics and categories, so they are easily searchable. If you ever need inspiration or knowledge related to your PCC, you should visit Tedtalks.com.

VISTAPRINT.COM

Vistaprint.com supplies custom business cards, flyers, brochures, hats, t-shirts, and more. For not very much money, you can have professional-looking marketing materials. I once used the site to order signs I stuck in the ground to advertise my weekly piano sales. At the end of your order, they always ask if you want pens, coffee mugs, paper weights, etc. with your company name and logo. Never underestimate the power of a refrigerator magnet with your company name and phone number: for some businesses, this is terrific advertising!

2. USE A BUDGET

For a while, I dreamt of becoming a famous painter. I felt inspired after I saw Monet's "Water Lilies" at the Chicago Institute of Art. I loved the way the paint seemed to flow and lay effortlessly on the canvas. I began making large canvases, some 4'x 5,' others as big as 5'x7.' I used a lot of paint, mostly blue and white, and I made more than 100 paintings. I tried to replicate the emotions I experienced when sailing; I called them "wind and water."

Several galleries in the Twin Cities put them on display and priced them for around $4,000 to $5,000. Because they took only twenty minutes for me to paint each one, I felt this venture had some real potential. Thinking big, I planned to move to New York and hold big art events. My friend Andy and I packed some of the paintings in the back of my truck and hit the road.

One of my 'wind and water' paintings I made in 2005.

We stopped in Chicago and decided to place some of my art in this city as well. After we found galleries to sell my art in Chicago, I began painting more art in our hotel room in preparation for New York. Andy would help gesso the canvases and paint around the edges, while I layered the paint. After three weeks, Andy missed his girlfriend too much and left for home. So I packed up the truck and drove straight through to New York.

When I finally got there, I realized I couldn't afford to live in New York without immediate income. I remember sitting in my hotel room's bathtub, realizing my dream could not happen. I had trouble breathing because I didn't know what to do, or where to turn. I eventually packed up my truck and drove home.

When I got home, I put myself on a strict $100 per month budget. I lived with my parents and kept track of every penny I spent. Although I no longer live on only $100 per month, I still keep a meticulous budget. Whenever I spend money, I make sure to keep the receipt and record it later in an Excel spreadsheet. If I am over budget for the month, I spread this overage over the next 12 months, and reduce my budget by that amount. This type of discipline helps ensure I always have money in the bank and avoids the stress of not having enough money to pay bills.

I also use a cash-flow projection sheet to plan for and anticipate future spending for K44K. I use this with my finance committee and it allows us to see how much cash we have on hand at any given point over the next fiscal year. This helps us prepare for slow sales periods and have enough money for payroll. In the summer months, we don't sell as many pianos, so it's important we plan for this and save money in our busier months. The cash-flow projection helps us organize reinvestment and growth strategies.

Realizing your PCC will require money. Make sure you manage your income and expenses and plan for the future.

3. KNOW VALUE

I bought my first cube van for moving pianos in 2009. I didn't have much money to invest, and I paid only $3,000 for the truck. I found a website and ordered black letters that said "Econo Piano Move," and I applied them to the side of the truck. The letters were pretty small, and they looked silly floating on the big white empty space on the box of the truck.

When it rained, water would pour into the cab through cracks in the ceiling. When it broke down, I would go on Craigslist and try to find mechanics to fix it as cheaply as possible. I even tried changing a few basic parts myself. I constantly spent money on repairs and paid hundreds of dollars each month. Often, the problem that should have been fixed broke again within a few days, or I couldn't find someone to make repairs before the following day's moves.

Eventually, I started to bring my truck to a real mechanic. He charged $91/hour, but the work was done right and on time. I could focus my energy on moving pianos and running a business, not finding belts for an alternator.

Eventually, the entire frame of the truck broke in half, and I had to sell it for scrap.

I replaced it with a newer, much nicer truck that I bought for $12,000. Although it cost more money, I have not put nearly the amount of money into repairs. When it does need a repair, I hire professional mechanics and I have much less stress dealing with breakdowns and rescheduling moving appointments.

Although a newer truck with low miles costs more upfront, and I can find cheaper, less experienced labor on Craigslist, in the long run it makes sense to invest in a quality truck and experienced, professional mechanics. When you are thinking about investing your own money into your PCC, think about what you get for your money. The cheapest option may not the best solution.

4. KNOW YOUR BUSINESS

You should have a working knowledge of all aspects of your PCC. In my business, I need to know how balance sheets work, but I also need to understand how to do a bridge repair on a grand piano. Even though I will never know exactly how the transmission on my truck works, it's nice to have a general idea. At the very least, I need to know how to check the fluid level and make sure the transmission gets flushed every 50,000 miles.

Last week, I tuned a piano for the first time in four years. I inspected the inside of it and adjusted key bushings on several sticking keys. I haven't worked on pianos for a long time, but it's nice to refresh these skills. It helps me run my business when I have a clear and fresh understanding of how each moving part of my business works.

Similar to how an adjustment of one piano part will affect how other parts interact with one another, it's important to have a basic knowledge of how all the moving parts of your PCC work together. It will help you make better, more informed decisions.

5. KNOW BASIC SALES SKILLS

We are all in the sales business. If we are not selling products to customers, we might be selling our business plan to an investor, or selling the value of an after-school program to a school, or selling ourselves to a potential partner.

Knowledge of basic sales skills will help you attract support, increase sales, and find greater success in your PCC. Plus, when the next salesperson tries to use a sales technique on you, you will be ready!

To be successful in sales, you have to understand people: their basic wants, desires, and behavior patterns. One nice thing about people is we are predictable.

When I expanded K44K to Kansas City, I hired a site manager named Bryce to run the business. Because we had a new location and didn't have much business, Bryce moved, fixed, and sold all the pianos by himself. A year after we opened our Kansas City location, we continued to show a loss each month.

I thought the poor sales might be due to our location. We had our business on the 3rd floor of a warehouse in a place called the West Bottoms. The main level of the building had no signage and customers had to climb a rickety set of stairs to see the pianos. In addition to this, the ceiling rained dust. Bryce had to constantly clean the pianos.

Hoping to revive piano sales, we moved our location to a warehouse with much better visibility and not nearly the same amount of dust. The new location cost more money, but we were willing to give it a shot. For six months after this move, we CONTINUED to see a loss of around $3,000 every month. Confused and frustrated, I couldn't seem to make a profit in Kansas City. The board became impatient and put pressure on me to either make a profit or shut down the location.

As a last effort, I hired a person named Leo to help Bryce sell. Leo had twenty-five years experience selling pianos, and he sold more than $10,000 of pianos during the first weekend. Since hiring Leo, Kansas City has been profitable every month, and I shared his sales techniques with the other two locations.

The sales techniques he uses can be found in a sales book called *The Art of Closing the Sale* by Brian Tracy. I recommend you study and read this book whether or not your PCC involves direct sales.

6. THINK AHEAD OF THE AIRPLANE

During my first flying lesson, my instructor, Mark, let me take off. There wasn't much to it. I moved a red throttle lever all the way forward, heard the choppy roar of a propeller blade, and gradually pulled the yoke (steering wheel) towards my chest. The front wheel began to skip up and down as this old bucket of metal fought to escape the clutches of gravity. The only thing kind of tricky about the whole process was to keep a slight pressure on the right pedal in order to counter the momentum of the propeller.

One of the first lessons Mark taught me was to *think ahead of the airplane.* I learned to anticipate future events, and to prepare for these well in advance, so I didn't need to rush or do things hastily at the last minute. While we were inbound for the airport, I would get weather reports and do pre-landing checks a good fifteen or twenty miles away from the airport. This allowed me the freedom to spend my time during the final approach scanning the sky for other airplanes and following air traffic instructions, instead of dealing with mixture settings and seatbelt checks.

I also tell my piano movers to "think ahead of the airplane." The process of moving pianos involves many steps. In order to move a piano successfully, a mover needs to plan and think about each of these steps. The first turn in the hallway might be navigated easily in any position, but the second turn in the staircase might need the piano to have the keys facing the outside wall so the piano can be flipped on the bottom edge, rotated, and swung into a strap. Each maneuver in the move must be anticipated, and each one affects every other aspect of the move.

Whether you are flying airplanes, moving pianos, or fulfilling some other task in life, anticipate and organize the process.

Think ahead of the airplane.

7. USE TO-DO LISTS

Thinking ahead of the airplane has to do with organization—organization of your time, processes, and surroundings. Organization helps you move effortlessly through your daily life and successfully meet challenges when they arise.

In real life, I don't use safety checklists like I do when I fly; instead, I use to-do lists. I have my to-do list organized in a Word document and I constantly delete, rearrange, and reference it throughout my day. I have one list about things I need to do today, one for things to do in the future, a list for things to bring up at the next finance meeting, and another list for things I need to buy the next time I'm at Target, etc.

When I think of something to add to this list, I use the voice memo app on my phone to create a recording of my thought. Every couple of days or so, I listen to the memos and type them into the Word document. By doing this, I don't need to waste energy remembering things, and nothing falls through the cracks.

Staying on top of all the many tasks and small jobs associated with your PCC will bring you success. Make lists and plan ahead of the airplane.

Here are some other ways to stay organized:

1. Use shelves, compartments, or boxes to organize all of your things. Use a label maker to clearly label all of these places.
2. Everything has a place, make sure you put it back when you are done using it.

3. Use a color-coded hanging filing system for your receipts and documents. I use the plastic ones because they are more durable.

4. Create folders on your computer that make sense to you, so you can easily find files and documents in the future.

5. Have your computer backed-up on a regular basis for WHEN it crashes in the future.

6. Keep all your books and study materials in one place so you can easily access and reference this material.

7. Have post-it notes handy so you can take notes while on the phone. Transfer these notes to your calendar or Word doc immediately so nothing gets lost or forgotten.

8. IF YOU ARE STUCK, WALK AWAY

I was at a home-improvement store the other day, trying to figure out how to display a sign at our Chicago warehouse. We needed a sign by the front door because when people arrived at the warehouse, they were confused and not sure if they were in the right place. Because the landlord doesn't allow us to put any signage on the building itself, I had to come up with a creative way to display the sign.

I debated whether or not to put plastic edges around it or screw it to a piece of plywood. When I looked at the plywood, I could buy the expensive or cheap version. The cheap version was warped. I didn't know if I should buy the treated plywood or if I should paint the normal version.

Pretty soon, I found myself sitting on one of those metal carts used for carrying lumber, with my face in my hands. I felt so frustrated and confused about how I should construct the display. I decided to drive to Chicago and figure it out when I got there.

I walked away.

While in Chicago the next day, I had a flash of creativity. Why not use the lid of an old grand piano to mount the sign? It would protect the metal edges, catch customers' eyes, and best of all, I could use materials I already had, saving money and the environment.

Sometimes creating space, sleeping on it, or walking away will help solve a nagging problem.

9. CALM YOUR NERVES

Earlier, I told you about how to "let go" of emotions that cause worry and stress. There is another kind of anxiety that has more to do with nerves that results in those pesky butterfly feelings.

A few months ago, I became a guest on a radio station in Chicago called WGN. The studio had several windows that overlooked downtown Chicago, and it felt as if I were speaking directly to the city itself—overwhelming! In order to stay calm, I used a terrific breathing technique that comes in handy when the butterflies start to flutter. It's simple. Take a deep breath in, hold it and count to four in your head, then exhale for another four seconds. Repeat until you feel relaxed and calm.

10. UTILIZE FACEBOOK

Facebook can be a great tool to help grow and market your PCC. There are some tricks I have learned over the years to help leverage this social media platform to your advantage.

You can create "pages" on Facebook for your PCC. These pages are just like your personal profile, but they are for a business. The goal is to get as many "likes" as possible and continually engage and keep the people who do "like" your page involved and interested. In order to do this, you should consistently update and manage your Facebook page.

SHARE CONTENT

One way to create more interest and appeal in your page is to share interesting content related to your PCC. When you find interesting articles or stories, share them as an update on your page. By sharing interesting content, you keep your followers engaged and help keep your PCC fresh in people's minds.

TAG PEOPLE IN PICTURE POSTS

When you post pictures on your page, make sure to tag people in the picture. This is a great way to encourage people to "like" your page. Hopefully, their friends will see this picture as well, and hopefully, they will "like" your page, too.

USE E-MAIL SIGNATURES

You can use your e-mail signature as a way to invite people to "like" your page. Underneath your name, put a link to your page and give them a reason to do it. We randomly give out free piano tunes to people who like our page, and we make sure to mention this in our e-mail signatures.

TRY USING FACEBOOK OFFERS

You can pay to put ads in the Ads dashboard on the right-hand column, but they are much more likely to be seen if you use something called Facebook offers. These offers appear in the normal news feed of Facebook. Make sure your offers are fun, unique, and something your followers will actually WANT. For example, we offer coupons for 50% off piano tuning.

11. LEVERAGE YOUR WEBSITE

Your website serves as a hub for your social media and online presence. As the Internet becomes further ingrained into the fabric of our society, your website will become more and more important. Make sure you utilize your website to its greatest potential.

BLOG

Just as with your Facebook page, it's important to remain active with your website. If you create a blog on your site, for example, you will give people a reason to visit your site and keep your PCC relevant, fresh, and interesting. A well-orchestrated blog drives new traffic to your site and improves the likelihood that someone will find you when using a search engine.

ASK THE AUDIENCE

Have a place on your website where people can engage and post their ideas and comments. When you give others a voice, they will be more likely to revisit your site and remain active with your PCC.

PROVIDE INFORMATION

If you can distinguish yourself as an expert and provide useful information on your site, you will attract more traffic. Make sure to have information on your site laid out in a simple, intuitive manner that allows visitors easy navigation.

12. ALWAYS CARRY BUSINESS CARDS

If this means you need to print your own cards or even write your contact information on a piece of paper, do it. You must have some way to give people you meet a way to reach you. You can buy sheets of blank business cards at an office supply store; make sure you get the ones that don't leave a perforated edge. As I mentioned before, Vistaprint.com is also a great place to order inexpensive cards.

Whenever you meet new people, make sure to give them your card. It's a good opportunity to ask them what they do and also to tell them about your exciting PCC. Make sure you explain what you do in a concise, clear, and interesting way. Some people call this an "elevator speech" because if you meet someone in an elevator, you don't have much time for a long conversation, so you need to be concise and brief.

You won't meet that many people in an elevator, but attention spans are about as short as a quick ride between floors, so you should have a quick, simple answer to the question: what do you do? Your answer should make the person want to learn more about what you do. It should be under ten seconds long.

Here is an example of my elevator speech:

"I inspire kids to believe in themselves by selling donated pianos and putting the profits toward music and art programs"

So what do you do?

_____

_____

_____

_____

_____

_____

_____

_____

I met a woman at a conference a few years ago. She asked questions about my business and we exchanged business cards. I didn't hear from her for about five weeks, but then out of the blue, she sent me an e-mail asking for a one-page summary of MUSE. As it turned out, a local foundation had hired this woman to find deserving nonprofits to receive grants. We eventually received a $24,000 grant a few months later because of a simple business card exchange.

Give out your business card, and talk to people you meet; you never know how you might work together in the future. After you have someone's card, make sure to follow up with them with a quick, friendly e-mail. Do this within a week so your meeting is still fresh in this person's mind. If it makes sense, invite them to coffee or lunch. Personal relationships open doors, cultivate growth, and help realize unseen potential for your PCC, so form as many as you can!

OCTAVE 7:

THINGS ARE WORKING; SOME ADVICE

"NOTHING GREAT WAS EVER ACHIEVED
WITHOUT ENTHUSIASM."

-RALPH WALDO EMERSON

1. DELEGATE

If you want to have the freedom to take breaks, see the big picture, be refreshed, and allow for creativity and passion in your work, you must delegate!

It's impossible to be good at everything and/or have time to do everything. I have a great bookkeeper named Dan who enters all of the sales receipts and does budgets for K44K. I am not a details person, and having someone do this is so valuable. I also have technicians to tune and repair pianos, salespeople to sell pianos, and movers to move pianos.

I actually like moving pianos. I like both the physical and mental challenge of each move. I like relaxing in a truck between jobs and being out in the real world. I think of each move as a new adventure: I never know who I will meet or what kind of house we will visit.

My job is not to move pianos, however. I have to delegate this and all other tasks in order to have the time to manage the business. I would miss opportunities if I immersed myself in tasks that should be delegated. I trust the people I hire, and I don't micromanage their work.

It's difficult to know when to hire others to do work you have done in the past. I use this checklist to know when this time comes:

1. Can I provide structure around how the work should be completed?
2. Am I missing opportunities by doing this work myself?
3. Can I afford to hire someone?
4. Is there enough work to make it worth while for someone?

In order for you to see success in your PCC, you will need to hire others to do jobs you did when you first started your PCC. This growth may come quickly or more gradually over the years, but it will come.

2. DON'T UNDERVALUE MOMENTUM

I often wonder what defined my PCC. Was it my website, the physical store, the literature and brochures, the articles of incorporation, or something else?

When I had to close MUSE due to lack of funding, I started to gain more perspective of my PCC.

After I closed the doors, my staff didn't have any work, so they left. The directors on my board didn't have anything to do, so they left. It quickly became me, sitting in the basement of my store, alone.

At this time, I had a fold-out table and a computer in the basement of my Minneapolis store. I remember thinking that nothing had changed. I still had all my file cabinets and brochures, a website, and a phone. My staff and board were gone, but I could find other people, right?

At the time, I thought *I* was the organization. I'm the one who formed it, worked hard, and made it what it had become. And if I was still here, my organization was too, right? I made a few calls to past contacts, telling them I planned to form a new board of directors. I called some past grantors to see if they wanted to support me. No one seemed interested.

That's when I realized I had lost my business. Things weren't the same. I realized my business was momentum, and I had lost my momentum. It was the momentum of ideas, shared by my board, employees, students, and the community as a whole. Websites, brochures, and business cards created the *structure* around this momentum, but at the end of the day, *people* carry momentum in their hearts and minds.

Momentum must be earned. I had lost momentum, and it took me another four years before I felt K44K had earned the same momentum I felt when MUSE existed. I have so much more appreciation for this momentum now, and I realize how fragile it can be.

As long as you have a clear vision of where you are going, and do so in an honest and patient way, momentum will be yours as well.

Cherish and protect it.

3. BE LOYAL

I have had the same accountant, Michele, for the last eight years. She makes visits to our office when we have questions, and she even comes in on Sundays.

She came in last week to prepare a balance sheet for us. I am the only client she visits outside her office. When she gives me advice, I know I can trust her because she understands my business and more importantly, she cares.

There will be people you know you can trust. These people will be by your side in both thick and thin. Show these people how much you appreciate them, and forgive them if they make mistakes.

The goal is not to find people who don't make mistakes, because everyone makes mistakes. The goal is to find people who care. From my experiences, the people who care about me personally are the ones who also care about my PCC.

I have known my friend Andy since we were ten years old. We had the same violin teacher and played together in a recital one spring. I wore a red bow tie, and we both had big dorky glasses. Andy doesn't get into the whole nonprofit thing, and even goes so far as to say in his will to specifically not give his money to charity. However, Andy has been a board member of K44K for the last three years and has attended almost every special event or fundraiser I have ever had.

Cherish these relationships.

4. FOCUS ON THE BENEFIT YOU PROVIDE

In order for a business to be successful, it needs to provide a product or service that benefits someone. In exchange for this benefit, the business makes money. Businesses need to realize that they create this benefit FIRST, and profit is a byproduct of this benefit. Businesses don't create money; they create products or services. Focus on these products and services that benefit others, and profit will naturally follow.

When I sell pianos to customers, I give them the best service possible. There is a difference between providing quality service and simply trying to sell pianos. If I were to focus only on selling pianos, the approach would be entirely different, and, I believe, less profitable in the long run. When I meet with customers, I try to listen to their needs.

Sometimes, I don't think I have a particular piano they want, and I recommend they visit another store.

Sometimes, I recommend they wait until their child shows more commitment to lessons before purchasing a piano.

Sometimes, it makes sense for a technician to assess their current piano to make sure it does, in fact, need to be replaced.

Although I might lose some sales in the near future, I believe in the long run, this type of customer focus builds a business as well as a community.

5. ENGAGE CUSTOMERS WITH MARKETING

If you want a successful marketing plan, you have to be unique. Your marketing campaign must grab the attention of your customer. Your marketing strategy should engage its audience; your customers should want to tell their friends about you.

Last year, K44K put twenty pianos around St. Paul in outdoor parks and sidewalks in a project called Pianos on Parade. The pianos were "artistically transformed" by local artists in a wide variety of colorful and creative ways. Several media sources covered Pianos on Parade from different human-interest angles. This press coverage promoted K44K, but in a way that engaged our audience. Traditional marketing becomes background static as people go about their day.

In order to rise above this static, engage your customers. Ask them questions, interact in unusual ways and in turn, they will grow and promote your PCC.

How will you engage your customers?

1. _____

2. _____

3. _____

4. _____

5. _____

6. _____

7. _____

8. _____

6. WORK WITH YOUR COMPETITION

I have a competitor who sells high-end pianos only two doors down from me. For the most part, this works out well because my pianos usually cost less than $1,000, so our stores together create a nice variety. When customers come to his store and want a more cost-effective option, they can walk over to us. If we don't have the type of piano someone wants, that customer can walk next door. Our block becomes a one-stop shopping for any type of piano.

Every year, I go to a meeting sponsored by the local movers association and meet with other household movers in the Twin Cities. We share stories, talk about trends, and discuss different marketing and moving techniques. Because I specialize in moving pianos, I often get referrals from these other companies that do only general household moves.

The word "competitor" has such negative connotations. How about we coin new terms like: "industry associates" or "fellow market professionals?"

Many opportunities exist for us to work together with our fellow *industry associates.* By working together, we can do a better job serving our customer base. When we do a good job serving our customers, we create repeat business; customers tell their friends, and business booms.

7. BE CHARITABLE

During my sophomore year at the U of M, I served on the student board of directors of the U-Y. Our main responsibility involved promoting and representing the U-Y to the larger U of M student body. I came up with a program called Subs in Tubs to accomplish this goal.

Subs in Tubs asked persons from the student population to come to the U-Y and make submarine sandwiches in an assembly line fashion. One sub would be for the person making it; the other would be put in plastic tubs and brought to local homeless shelters. At first, I donated $1,000 of my own money to pay for the meat, cheese, bread, and other supplies. We did the event a couple of times, and we had around one hundred people show up each time. We filled one large tub during each event and brought the sandwiches to a local homeless shelter in Minneapolis.

After the second event, someone from our committee suggested we start charging $5 per person. In addition to the sub, we would provide chips and a drink. We networked with the U of M and asked if we could be a part of their spring event called Spring Jam. They said yes and allowed us to set up tables at the end of a bridge connecting the east and west campus.

We printed a banner, complete with a logo of a sub character riding in a tub and giving a thumbs-up sign. We printed brochures and advertised in the campus paper. On the day of the event, we had more than 700 people show up and not only did we donate more than 700 subs to homeless shelters, we also paid for all of our expenses, plus generated a profit of more than $1,000 for the U-Y. We held several more Subs in Tubs events at the U of M over the next two years, with continued success.

I believe a large part of our success can be attributed to our charitable purpose. If you can define and explain a charitable purpose, or incorporate a charitable cause into your PCC, I believe you will increase your chances for success.

Describe how your PCC could be charitable:

1. _____

2. _____

3. _____

4. _____

5. _____

6. _____

One of the Subs in Tubs events at the
University of Minnesota in 2003.

8. USE KICKSTARTER TO FIND START-UP MONEY

I recently visited a group of islands off the cost of Panama called Bocas del Toro. Clear waters, coral reefs, and even an occasional dolphin sighting made this an unforgettable vacation.

I stayed in a hostel one night that had only recently opened for business. A woman named Pascal moved from New York to start her business with two of her friends. (Can you say *PCC*?) The group raised $15,000 to fund the project by posting a video on kickstarter.com.

Kickstarter helps people with brilliant ideas raise needed capital for new business ventures or creative projects. Money raised on the site can be used to pay for development, production, and distribution costs for their ideas. Inventors post a video on the website explaining their idea and capital goal. In exchange for investing in these ideas, visitors to the site receive various things from the inventor.

For example, people investing $20 in Pascal's idea received a T-shirt she designed. People investing $500 received a free, all-inclusive one-week stay for two people in the hostel.

If your PCC involves a product, or if you have something you can give people in exchange for investing in your idea, this might be a great way to "kick start" your PCC.

Things you could give to investors on Kickstarter:

1. _____

2. _____

3. _____

4. _____

5. _____

6. _____

9. INVOLVE YOUR COMMUNITY

My St. Paul store is located in a vibrant community with a mix of both retail and residential properties. Each year, the Grand Avenue Business Association (GABA) holds several events on the avenue. There is a day called Paws on Grand which encourages people to bring their animals to stores and shops on Grand Avenue. There is also something called Grand Meander, a Halloween holiday event called Boo Bash, and the largest of the events, Grand Old Days.

Grand Old Days closes the street to vehicular traffic for an entire day and draws more than 250,000 people. The festival includes a parade in the morning and events and entertainment in the afternoon. Children ride ponies and jump in bouncy castles, and adults listen to live music and drink beer.

Find unique and fun ways to involve your local community, and you will find greater success in your PCC. Your community wants to support local ventures, so give them an avenue to walk down for a day!

Think about how you can involve your community:

1. _____

2. _____

3. _____

4. _____

5. _____

6. _____

7. _____

8. _____

10. DOCUMENT YOUR MODEL

You might not always be on site to tell someone how things should be done. It's your PCC, and you know the process you want to use better than anyone else. Document your system and organize it in such a way that someone can easily replicate it.

I use a binder with various tabs and sections. Some sections talk about specific tips on how to move a piano. Other sections explain what to say to donors when they call to donate a piano. The idea is that I can hand this binder to someone in city X and this person can start another K44K with as much quality as if I were there helping them.

There's a lot of pieces that need to come together to achieve your vision. I believe your PCC should become something bigger than you. Your vision may need to be replicated by others. Tell them how.

11. TEACH AND ENCOURAGE OTHERS

After you have created a PCC that rewards you beyond your wildest dreams, help others do the same.

People need encouragement. Encourage them.

People need support. Support them.

People need validation. Validate them.

As a mentor in the Y-Buddies program, I saw the excitement in the eyes of my mentee when I took him to a monster-truck rally. I remember the long pauses separated by moments of epiphany when he understood math problems. I can assure you, helping others discover their passions and talents will reward and enrich your own life.

We share this world together for a short time. Let's help each other and open the floodgates for love and joy.

12. REINVEST YOUR MONEY

When your PCC generates profit and you have decisions to make about how to use this extra cash, think about these three words: *Return on Investment* (ROI). Ask yourself, where will you get the greatest ROI, and put your money there. You can calculate ROI by dividing the amount of income the investment would generate in a year and divide it by the total cost of the investment.

I make lists of uses for extra money, and assign approximate ROI next to each one. The expenses with the greatest ROI become my priority, and the lesser ones get put to the bottom of the list.

Printing business cards, flyers, or other printed materials usually has a high ROI because they are cheap to produce and often result in valuable leads or sales. Fixed assets, like vehicles or equipment, generate cash and retain a high percentage of their value, so these are also good investments with high ROI. Real estate offers added benefits because of the appreciation potential. And, you guessed it: a new Lexus or Prada sunglasses have a low ROI.

In addition to putting capital in high-ROI investments, it's also a good idea to put cash away for a rainy day. A safe amount would be around six months of expenses. This savings will cover slow months or unforeseen expenses.

OCTAVE 8:
CLOSING THOUGHTS

"GO CONFIDENTLY IN THE DIRECTION OF YOUR DREAMS. LIVE THE LIFE YOU HAVE IMAGINED."

-HENRY DAVID THOREAU

1. BE GRATEFUL

I t takes less effort to appreciate what you have than to obtain what you THINK will make you happy. If you can't be content in this moment, you never will, no matter how much you accomplish. It's a fact: be grateful in the present, and you will forever be content and at peace.

As I mentioned earlier, I want to expand K44K to fifty cities around the United States. A few years ago, I also had this same goal, but this goal got in the way of my ability to be content in the present. I had the belief that I could not be happy unless my business existed in multiple cities around the county.

One day, I closed my eye and imagined all the things I wanted to accomplish. I imagined all the moving parts of the business coming together and the excitement and pride I felt. I allowed the feelings to crash over me like a salty ocean wave and consume my awareness. I allowed this feeling to linger in my consciousness and asked the question,

"Could I allow myself to have these same feelings NOW?"

Why should I limit feelings of gratitude and pride, if I could welcome them into my life NOW?

When we welcome feelings of gratitude into our awareness, we attract more things into our lives that give us gratitude. We lose our sunglasses, we look for our sunglasses, and eventually we find them. Our subconscious works the same way. If we fill our subconscious with fear and frustration, we will find and attract things that scare and frustrate us. In contrast, if we fill our subconscious with feelings of joy and gratitude, you guessed it: we find things that give us joy and gratitude.

2. THE NEW NONPROFIT

I have spent the majority of my PCC in the nonprofit sector and have some ideas and insight I would like to share. Nonprofits represent an enormous force for good in our society, and I want to see them function to their fullest potential.

Because nonprofits provide goods and services to constituents often for free or reduced fees, they rely on outside funding and donations to support charitable activities. The donations, however, can be unpredictable, restrictive, and almost always not enough.

Nonprofits shouldn't need to adjust their charitable activities in order to satisfy granting requirements and wonder each year how many grants and donation checks will come through the mailbox slot. I imagine a new kind of nonprofit that has freedom to focus its energy and resources in specific and measurable ways and not have the traditional funding uncertainties and distractions.

Am I an unrealistic optimist? Maybe. Especially if these words came from the twenty-year-old who showed up to the Rondo school in St. Paul in 2001 with a handful of electronic keyboards and some color crayons. After thirteen years in the nonprofit field, however, I have many rich experiences that reinforce this opinion.

Nonprofits can and must find creative ways to engage their communities and generate alternative funding sources. Ideally, these sources would align with the nonprofit's mission and current products or services. Nonprofits have marketable expertise, skills, and products that can easily overlap and exist in for-profit, consumer markets. By bridging the divide between traditional for-profit and non-profit sectors, we create stronger, more independent, and fiscally sound nonprofits, and in turn, stronger communities.

There's nothing wrong with providing terrific, mission-based services and in turn asking the local community for donation dollars, but take control of your nonprofit.

Don't rely on these donation dollars each year; instead, find ways to generate capital with your expertise.

Also, don't be afraid to reinvest capital back into your nonprofit. You may need to delay some charitable aspects of your nonprofit for a few years, but in the end, you will have a stronger, more fiscally sound organization that can reach larger numbers of constituents and achieve greater impact.

3. SHARE YOUR STORY

Visit the website www.octavesofsuccess.com and share your experiences, frustrations, failures, and successes as you take the leap and create your PCC. We can support each other as we forge new paths and realize our true potential.

I am excited to hear all about your wonderful stories, ideas, hopes, and dreams. I believe the world will be a better place because of YOU!

In my next book, *Octaves of Success: 88 Stories of Hope and Inspiration*, I will highlight eighty-eight readers and your stories of transformation and PCC realization. Who knows, you might be one of the eighty-eight!

4. CREATE YOUR OWN KEY

Create your own "key" to success below. Share this key on our website, **www.octavesofsuccess.com** and have a chance to win a free consultation with me!

_____

_____

_____

_____

_____

_____

_____

_____

_____

_____

ABOUT THE AUTHOR

NEWELL H. HILL

As a child I built tree forts and go-carts and dreamt about exploring distant planets. I have always enjoyed pushing the limits of my creativity and testing boundaries of the status quo. As an adult I have started over ten companies and carry the entrepreneurial torch proudly. I am a recipient of the David M. Wallace Award for Creativity and believe each of us have gifts to share with the world if we let our passions fly free.

ACKNOWLEDGMENTS

I want to thank Kelsey for her inspiration to write this book. I think her passion for books and literature must have rubbed off on me while we worked together from 2010-12. I also want to thank her for all her terrific content and copy edits, as well as holding my hand through the publishing process.

I also want to thank my parents as well as Ruth for helping with final edits. And thank you to Annie for designing a great cover and swimming through a sea of post-it notes.

And to Jill for staying up past her bedtime to make sure all my i's had dots and my t's had horizontal lines running through them.

NOTES:

NOTES: